Preface

The aim of this textbook is to provide detailed coverage of the topics in the new AQA A Level Computer Science specification.

The book is divided into six sections and within each section, each chapter covers material that can comfortably be taught in one or two lessons.

In the second year of this course there is a strong emphasis on algorithms and data structures, and these are covered in the first two sections of the book. These are followed by sections on regular languages, the Internet and databases.

Object Oriented Programming and functional programming are covered in the final section, which describes basic theoretical concepts in OOP, as well as providing some practical exercises using the functional programming language Haskell. Lists, the fact-based model and 'Big Data' are all described and explained.

Two short appendices contain A Level content that could be taught in the first year of the course as an extension to related AS topics.

The OOP concepts covered may also be helpful in the coursework element of the A Level course.

Each chapter contains exercises and questions, some new and some from past examination papers. Answers to all these are available to teachers only in a Teacher's Supplement which can be ordered from our website **www.pgonline.co.uk**.

Approval message from AQA

This textbook has been approved by AQA for use with our qualification. This means that we have checked that it broadly covers the specification and we are satisfied with the overall quality. Full details of our approval process can be found on our website.

We approve textbooks because we know how important it is for teachers and students to have the right resources to support their teaching and learning. However, the publisher is ultimately responsible for the editorial control and quality of this book.

Please note that when teaching the A Level Computer Science course, you must refer to AQA's specification as your definitive source of information. While this book has been written to match the specification, it cannot provide complete coverage of every aspect of the course.

A wide range of other useful resources can be found on the relevant subject pages of our website: www.aqa.org.uk.

Contents

Section 7

Data structures

In this section:

7

Chapter 37 – Queues

Objectives

- Understand the concept of an abstract data type
- Be familiar with the concept and uses of a queue
- Describe the creation and maintenance of data within a queue (linear, circular, priority)
- Describe and apply the following to a linear, circular and priority queue
    - add an item
    - remove an item
    - test for an empty queue
    - test for a full queue

Introduction to data structures

Programming languages such as Python, Visual Basic or Java all have built-in **elementary data types** such as integer, real, Boolean and char, and some built-in **composite data types** such as string, array or list, for example.

Abstract data types such as queues, stacks, trees and graphs can easily be shown in graphical form, and it is not hard to understand how to perform operations such as adding, deleting or counting elements in each structure. However, programming languages require data types to represent them. An abstract data type (**ADT**) is a logical description of how the data is viewed and the operations that can be performed on it, but how this is to be done is not necessarily known to the user. It is up to the programmer who creates the data structure to decide how to implement it, and it may be built in to the programming language. This is a good example of **data abstraction**, and by providing this level of abstraction we are creating an **encapsulation** around the data, hiding the details of implementation from the user. This is called **information hiding**.

As a programmer, you will be quite familiar with this concept. When you call a built-in function such as `random` to generate a random number, or `sqrt` to find the square root of a number, you are not at all concerned with how these functions are implemented.

Queues

A queue is a **First In First Out (FIFO)** data structure. New elements may only be added to the end of a queue, and elements may only be retrieved from the front of a queue. The sequence of data items in a queue is determined, therefore, by the order in which they are inserted. The size of the queue depends on the number of items in it, just like a queue at traffic lights or at a supermarket checkout.

Queues are used in a variety of applications:

- Output waiting to be printed is commonly stored in a queue on disk. In a room full of networked computers, several people may send work to be printed at more or less the same time. By putting the output into a queue on disk, the output is printed on a first come, first served basis as soon as the printer is free.

- Characters typed at a keyboard are held in a queue in a keyboard buffer.

- Queues are useful in simulation problems. A simulation program is one which attempts to model a real-life situation so as to learn something about it. An example is a program that simulates customers arriving at random times at the check-outs in a supermarket store, and taking random times to pass through the checkout. With the aid of a simulation program, the optimum number of check-out counters can be established.

Operations on a queue

The abstract data type **queue** is defined by its structure and the operations which can be performed on it. It is described as an ordered collection of items which are added at the rear of the queue, and removed from the front.

When Eli leaves the queue, the front pointer is made to point to Jason; the elements themselves do not move. When Adam joins the queue, the rear pointer points to Adam. Think of a queue in a doctor's surgery – people leave and join the queue, but no one moves chairs.

The following queue operations are needed:

- enQueue(item)   Add a new item to the rear of the queue
- deQueue()   Remove the front item from the queue and return it
- isEmpty()   Test to see whether the queue is empty
- isFull()   Test to see whether queue is full

7-37

Q1: Complete the following table to show the queue contents and the value returned by the function or **method**. The queue is named **q**.

Queue operation	Queue contents	Return value
q.isEmpty()	[]	True
q.enQueue("Blue")	["Blue"]	(none)
q.enQueue("Red")	["Blue", "Red"]	
q.enQueue("Green")		
q.isFull()		False
q.isEmpty()	["Blue", "Red", "Green"]	
q.deQueue()		
q.enQueue("Yellow")		

Dynamic vs static data structures

A **dynamic data structure** refers to a collection of data in memory that has the ability to grow or shrink in size. It does this with the aid of the **heap**, which is a portion of memory from which space is automatically allocated or de-allocated as required.

Languages such as Python, Java and C support dynamic data structures, such as the built-in `list` data type in Python.

Dynamic data structures are very useful for implementing data structures such as queues when the maximum size of the data structure is not known in advance. The queue can be given some arbitrary maximum to avoid causing memory overflow, but it is not necessary to allocate space in advance.

A **static data structure** such as a static array is fixed in size, and cannot increase in size or free up memory while the program is running. An array is suitable for storing a fixed number of items such as the months of the year, monthly sales or average monthly temperatures. The disadvantage of using an array to implement a dynamic data structure such as a queue is that the size of the array has to be decided in advance by the programmer, and if the number of items added fills up the array, then no more can be added, regardless of how much free space there is in memory. Python does not have a built-in `array` data structure. A further disadvantage is that memory which has been allocated to the array cannot be reallocated even if most of it is unused. However, an advantage of a static data structure is that no pointers or other data about the structure need to be stored, in contrast to a dynamic data structure.

Implementing a linear queue

There are basically two ways to implement a linear queue in an array or list:

1. As items leave the queue, all of the other items move up one space so that the front of the queue is always the first element of the structure, e.g. q[0]. With a long queue, this may require significant processing time.

2. A linear queue can be implemented with pointers to the front and rear of the queue. An integer holding the size of the array (the maximum size of the queue) is needed, as well as a variable giving the number of items currently in the queue. However, clearly a problem will arise as many items are added to and deleted from the queue, as space is created at the front of the queue which cannot be filled, and items are added until the rear pointer points to the last element of the data structure.

> **Q2:** The queue of names pictured above containing Jason, Milly, Bob and Adam has space for six names. What will be the situation when Jason and Milly leave the queue, and Jack joins it? How many names are now in the queue? How many free spaces are left?

A circular queue

One way of overcoming the limitations of implementing a queue as a linear queue is to use a **circular queue** instead, so that when the array fills up and the rear pointer points to the last element of the array, say q[5], it will be made to point to the first element, q[0], when the next person joins the queue, assuming this element is empty. This solution requires some extra effort on the part of the programmer, and is less flexible than a dynamic data structure if the maximum number of items is not known in advance.

7-37

Q3: A circular queue is implemented in a fixed size array of six elements, indexed from 0. Show the contents of the queue and the front and rear pointers for a circular queue of 6 items when

   (a)   it is empty

   (b)   Ali, Ben, Charlie, Davina, Enid, Fred join the queue. Ali, Ben and Charlie leave, and Greg joins the queue.

Pseudocode for implementing a circular queue

To initialise the queue:

```
SUB initialise
   front ← 0
   rear ← -1
   size ← 0
   maxSize ← size of array
ENDSUB
```

To test for an empty queue:

```
SUB isEmpty
   IF size = 0 THEN
      RETURN True
   ELSE
      RETURN False
   ENDIF
ENDSUB
```

To test for a full queue:

```
SUB isFull
   IF size = maxSize THEN
      RETURN True
   ELSE
      RETURN False
   ENDIF
ENDSUB
```

To add an element to the queue:

```
SUB enqueue(newItem)
   IF isFull THEN
      OUTPUT "Queue full"
   ELSE
      rear ← (rear + 1) MOD maxSize
      q[rear] ← newItem
      size ← size + 1
   ENDIF
ENDSUB
```

7-37

> **Q4:** In what respect is a circular queue an example of **abstraction**?

To remove an item from the queue:

```
SUB dequeue
   IF isEmpty THEN
      OUTPUT "Queue empty"
      item ← Null
   ELSE
      item ← q[front]
      front ← (front + 1) MOD maxSize
      size ← size - 1
   ENDIF
   RETURN item
ENDSUB
```

Priority queues

In some situations where items are placed in a queue, a system of priorities is used. For example an operating system might schedule jobs in order of priority, or a printer may give shorter print jobs priority over longer ones.

A **priority queue** acts like a queue in that items are dequeued by removing them from the front of the queue. However, the logical order of items within the queue is determined by their priority, with the highest priority items at the front of the queue and the lowest priority items at the back. It is therefore possible that a new item joins the queue at the front, rather than at the rear.

> **Q5:** In what circumstances would an item join a priority queue at the front? In what circumstances would the item join the queue at the rear?

Such a queue could be implemented by checking the priority of each item in the queue, starting at the rear and moving it along one place until an item with the same or lower priority is found, at which point the new item can be inserted.

An example of how to do this is included in the next chapter on Lists.

Exercises

1. (a)   Explain why a queue may be implemented as a **circular queue**.   [2]

   (b)   Explain what is meant by a **dynamic data structure** and why an inbuilt dynamic data structure in a programming language may be useful in implementing a queue.

         Include an explanation of what is meant by the **heap** in this context.   [4]

   (c)   Print jobs are put in a queue to be printed. The queue is implemented in an array, indexed from 0, as a circular queue which can hold 5 jobs. Jobs enter the queue in the sequence Job1, Job2, Job3, Job4, Job5. Pointers **front** and **rear** point to the first and last items in the queue respectively.

         (i)   Draw a diagram to show how the print jobs are stored. Include pointers in your diagram.   [3]

         (ii)   Two jobs are printed and leave the queue. Another job, Job6 joins the queue.

               Draw a diagram representing the new situation.   [2]

7-37

2. A computer program is being developed to play a card game on a smartphone. The game uses a standard deck of 52 playing cards, placed in a pile on top of each other.

The cards will be dealt (ie given out) to players from the top of the deck.

When a player gives up a card it is returned to the bottom of the deck.

(a) Explain why a queue is a suitable data structure to represent the deck of cards in this game.   [1]

(b) The queue representing the deck of cards will be implemented as a **circular** queue in a fixed size array named DeckQueue. The array DeckQueue has indices running from 1 to 52.

Figure 1 shows the contents of the DeckQueue array and its associated pointers at the start of a game. The variable QueueSize indicates how many cards are currently represented in the queue.

Figure 1

DeckQueue

Index	Data
[1]	10 – Hearts
[2]	2 – Spades
[3]	King – Hearts
[4]	Ace – Clubs
.	
.	
.	
[52]	8 – Diamonds

FrontPointer = 1

RearPointer = 52

QueueSize = 52

(i) Ten cards are dealt from the top of the deck.

What values are now stored in the FrontPointer and RearPointer pointers and the QueueSize variable?   [1]

(ii) Next, a player gives up two cards and these are returned to the deck.

What values are now stored in the FrontPointer and RearPointer pointers and the QueueSize variable?   [1]

(iii) Write a pseudo-code algorithm to deal a card from the deck.

Your algorithm should output the value of the card that is to be dealt and make any required modifications to the pointers and to the QueueSize variable.

It should also cope appropriately with any situation that might arise in the DeckQueue array whilst a game is being played.   [6]

AQA Unit 3 Qu 5 June 2014

Chapter 38 – Lists

Objectives

- Explain how a list may be implemented as either a static or dynamic data structure
- Show how items may be added to or deleted from a list

Definition of a list

In computer science, a **list** is an abstract data type consisting of a number of items in which the same item may occur more than once. The list is sequenced so that we can refer to the first, second, third,… item and we can also refer to the last element of the list.

A list is a very useful data type for a wide variety of operations, and can be used, for example, to implement other data structures such as a queue, stack or tree. Some languages such as Python have a built-in list data type, so that for example a list of numbers could be shown as

$$[45, \ 13, \ 19, \ 13, \ 8]$$

Q1: In a programming language which does not include the list data type, how could a list be implemented?

7-38

Operations on lists

Some possible list operations are shown in the following table. The list a is assumed to hold the values [45, 13, 19, 13, 8] initially, with the first element referred to as a[0].

List operation	Description	Example	list contents	Return value
isEmpty()	Test for empty list	a.isEmpty()	[45, 13, 19, 13, 8]	False
append(item)	Add a new item to list to the end of the list	a.append(33)	[45, 13, 19, 13, 8, 33]	
remove(item)	Remove the first occurrence of an item from list	a.remove(13)	[45, 19, 13, 8, 33]	
search(item)	Search for an item in list	a.search(22)	[45, 19, 13, 8, 33]	False
length()	Return the number of items	a.length()	[45, 19, 13, 8, 33]	5
index(item)	Return the position of item	a.index(8)	[45, 18, 13, 8, 33]	3
insert(pos,item)	Insert a new item at position pos	a.insert(2,7)	[45, 18, 7, 13, 8, 33]	
pop()	Remove and return the last item in the list	a.pop()	[45, 18, 7, 13, 8]	33
pop(pos)	Remove and return the item at position pos	a.pop(1)	[45, 7, 13, 8]	18

Q2: Assume that list names holds the values James, Paul, Sophie, Holly, Nathan.

What does the list hold after each of the following consecutive operations?

(i)　`names.append("Tom")`

(ii)　`names.pop(3)`

(iii)　`names.insert(1, "Melissa")`

Using an array

It is possible to maintain an ordered collection of data items using a static array, which is a static data structure. This may be an option if the programming language does not support the `list` data type and if the maximum number of data items is small, and is known in advance.

The programmer then has to work out and code algorithms for each list operation. The empty array must be declared in advance as being a particular length, and this could be used, for example, to hold a priority queue.

Inserting a new name in the list

If the list needs to be held in sequential order in the array, the algorithm will first have to determine where a new item has to be added, and then if necessary, move the rest of the items along in order to make room for it.

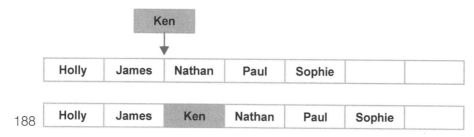

188

The steps are as follows:

```
Test for list already full, print message if it is and quit
Determine where new item needs to be inserted
Starting at the end of the list, move other items along one place
Insert new item in correct place
```

Q3: Suggest a different algorithm for adding a new element to a sequenced list.

Q4: How could the given algorithm be adapted to insert an item in a priority queue?

Deleting a name from the list

Suppose the name Ken is to be deleted from the list shown below. The names coming after Ken in the list need to be moved up to fill the gap.

Holly	James	Ken	Nathan	Paul	Sophie	

Q5: Why not simply leave the array element names[2] blank after deleting *Ken*?

First, items are moved up to fill the empty space by copying them to the previous spot in the array:

Holly	James	Nathan	Paul	Sophie	Sophie	

7-38

Finally the last element, which is now duplicated, is replaced with a blank.

Holly	James	Nathan	Paul	Sophie		

Using a dynamic data structure to implement an ordered list

Programming languages such as Python have a built-in dynamic `list` data structure which is internally implemented using a **linked list**. Functional abstraction hides all the details of how all the associated functions and methods are implemented, making the programmer's task much easier! As items are added to the list, the pointers are adjusted to point to new memory locations taken from the heap. When items are deleted, pointers are again adjusted and the freed-up memory is de-allocated and returned to the heap.

As new nodes are added, new memory locations can be dynamically pulled from the **heap**, a pool of memory locations which can be allocated or deallocated as required. The pointers then need to be changed to maintain the correct sequence.

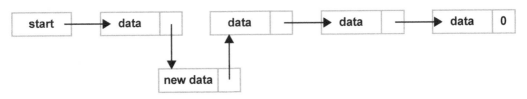

7-38

The following shows an interactive session in Python:

```
>>> names = ['James', 'Paul', 'Sophie', 'Holly', 'Nathan']
>>> names
['James', 'Paul', 'Sophie', 'Holly', 'Nathan']
>>> len(names)
5
>>> names.append('Tom')
>>> names
['James', 'Paul', 'Sophie', 'Holly', 'Nathan', 'Tom']
>>> names.pop(3)
'Holly'
>>> names
['James', 'Paul', 'Sophie', 'Nathan', 'Tom']
>>> names.insert(1,'Melissa')
>>> names
['James', 'Melissa', 'Paul', 'Sophie', 'Nathan', 'Tom']
```

Note that append, pop and insert are **methods** on a list object, while len() is a **function** that takes the list as an argument.

Exercises

1. A list data structure can be represented using an array.

The pseudocode algorithm in Figure 1 can be used to carry out one useful operation on a list.

Figure 1

```
p ← 1
If ListLength > 0 Then
    While p <= ListLength And List[p] < New Do
        p ← p + 1
    EndWhile
    For q ← ListLength DownTo p Do
        List[q + 1] ← List[q]
    EndFor
EndIf
List[p] ← New
ListLength ← ListLength + 1
```

(a) The initial values of the variables for one particular execution of the algorithm are shown in the trace table below, labelled Table 1.

Complete the trace table for the execution of the algorithm.

Table 1

				List				
ListLength	**New**	**p**	**q**	**[1]**	**[2]**	**[3]**	**[4]**	**[5]**
4	38	–	–	9	21	49	107	

[4]

(b) Describe the purpose of the algorithm in Figure 1. [1]

(c) A list implemented using an array is a static data structure. The list could be implemented using a linked list as a dynamic data structure instead.

    (i) Describe one difference between a static data structure and a dynamic data structure. [1]

    (ii) If the list were to be implemented as a dynamic data structure, explain what the heap would be used for. [1]

AQA Unit 3 Qu 10 June 2010

Chapter 39 – Stacks

Objectives

- Be familiar with the concept and uses of a stack

- Be able to describe the creation and maintenance of data within a stack

- Be able to describe and apply the following operations: push, pop, peek (or top), test for empty stack, test for full stack

- Be able to explain how a stack frame is used with subroutine calls to store return addresses, parameters and local variables

Concept of a stack

A **stack** is a Last In, First Out (**LIFO**) data structure. This means that, like a stack of plates in a cafeteria, items are added to the top and removed from the top.

Applications of stacks

A stack is an important data structure in Computing. Stacks are used in calculations, and to hold return addresses when subroutines are called. When you use the **Back** button in your Web browser, you will be taken back through the previous pages that you looked at, in reverse order as their URLs are removed from the stack and reloaded. When you use the **Undo** button in a word processing package, the last operation you carried out is popped from the stack and undone.

Implementation of a stack

A stack may be implemented as either a **static** or **dynamic** data structure.

A static data structure such as an **array** can be used with two additional variables, one being a pointer to the top of the stack and the other holding the size of the array (the maximum size of the stack).

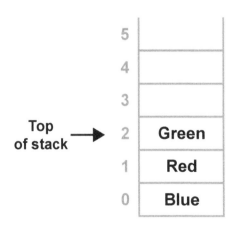

Operations on a stack

The following operations are required to implement a stack:

- push(item)   adds a new item to the top of the stack
- pop()   removes and returns the top item from the stack
- peek()   returns the top item from the stack but does not remove it
- isEmpty()   tests to see whether the stack is empty, and returns a Boolean value
- isFull()   tests to see whether the stack is full, and returns a Boolean value

Stack operation	Stack contents	Return value
s.isEmpty()	[]	True
s.push('Blue')	['Blue']	
s.push('Red')	['Blue', 'Red']	
s.push('Green')	['Blue', 'Red', 'Green']	
s.isEmpty	['Blue', 'Red', 'Green']	False
s.peek()	['Blue', 'Red', 'Green']	'Green'
s.pop()	['Blue', 'Red']	'Green'

The following pseudocode implements four of the stack operations using a fixed size array.

```
SUB isEmpty
   IF top = -1 THEN
      RETURN True
   ELSE
      RETURN False
   ENDIF
ENDSUB

SUB isFull
   IF top = maxSize THEN
      RETURN True
   ELSE
      RETURN False
   ENDIF
ENDSUB

SUB push(item)
   IF isFull THEN
      OUTPUT "Stack is full"
   ELSE
      top ← top + 1
      s(top)← item
   ENDIF
ENDSUB
```

7-39

```
SUB pop
   IF isEmpty THEN
      OUTPUT "Stack is empty"
   ELSE
      item ← s(top)
      top ← top - 1
   ENDIF
ENDSUB
```

Q1: Write pseudocode for a "peek" subroutine.

Q2: Show the state of the stack and stack pointer after the following operations have been performed on the stack containing ('Blue', 'Red'):

(i)   Pop

(ii) Pop

(iii) Push('Yellow')

Some languages, such as Python, make it very easy to implement a stack using the built-in dynamic `list` data structure, with the top of the stack being the last element of the list.

The function `len(s)` can be used to determine whether the stack is empty, and if it is not, `pop()` will remove and return the top (last) element. The built-in method `append(item)` will append or push an item onto the top of the stack (the last element of the list).

7-39

Overflow and underflow

A stack will always have a maximum size, because memory cannot grow indefinitely. If the stack is implemented as an array, a full stack can be tested for by examining the value of the stack pointer. An attempt to push another item onto the stack would cause **overflow** so an error message can be given to the user to avoid this. Similarly, if the stack pointer is -1, the stack is empty and **underflow** will occur if an attempt is made to pop an item.

Functions of a call stack

A major use of the stack data structure is to store information about the active subroutines while a computer program is running. The details are hidden from the user in all high level languages.

Holding return addresses

The **call stack** keeps track of the address of the instruction that control should return to when a subroutine ends (the **return address**). Several subroutines may be nested, so that the stack may contain several return addresses which will be popped as each subroutine completes. For example, a subroutine which draws a robot may call subroutines `drawCircle`, `drawRectangle` etc. Subroutine `drawRectangle` may in turn call a subroutine `drawLine`.

A recursive subroutine may contain several calls to itself, so that with each call, a new item (the return address) is pushed onto the stack. When the recursion finally ends, the return addresses that have been pushed onto the stack each time the routine is called are popped one after the other, each time the end of the subroutine is reached. If the programmer makes an error and the recursion never ends, sooner or later memory will run out, the stack will overflow and the program will crash.

Holding parameters

Parameters required for a subroutine (such as, for example, the centre coordinates, line colour and thickness for a circle subroutine) may be held on the call stack. Each call to a subroutine will be given separate space on the call stack for these values.

Local variables

A subroutine frequently uses local variables which are known only within the subroutine. These may also be held in the call stack. Each separate call to a subroutine gets its own space for its local variables. Storing local variables on the call stack is much more efficient than using dynamic memory allocation, which uses **heap** space.

The stack frame

A call stack is composed of **stack frames**. Each stack frame corresponds to a call to a subroutine which has not yet terminated.

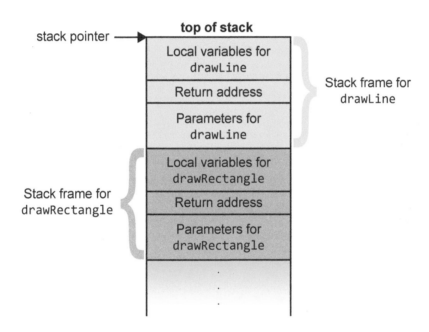

7-39

Exercises

1. A Last In, First Out (LIFO) data structure has a pointer called **top**.

   (a) What is this type of data structure known as?   [1]

   (b) Name and briefly describe one type of error that could occur when attempting to add a data item or remove a data item from the data structure.   [2]

   (c) Describe briefly one use of this type of data structure in a computer system.   [2]

   (d) Write a pseudocode procedure for reversing the elements of a queue with the aid of a stack.   [6]

Chapter 40 – Hash tables and dictionaries

Objectives

- Be familiar with a hash table and its uses

- Be able to apply simple hashing algorithms

- Know what is meant by a collision and how collisions are handled using rehashing

- Be familiar with the concept of a dictionary

- Be familiar with simple applications of a dictionary

Hashing

Large collections of data, for example customer records in a database, need to be accessible very quickly without having to look through all the records. This can be done by holding an **index** of the physical address on the file where the data is held. But how is the index created?

The answer is that a **hashing algorithm** is applied to the value in the key field of each record to transform it into an address. Normally there are many more possible keys than actual records that need to be stored. For example, suppose 300 records are to be stored, each having a unique 6-digit identifier or key, and 1000 free spaces have been allocated to store the records.

One common hashing algorithm is to divide the key by the number of available addresses and take the remainder as the address. Using the algorithm (address = key mod 1000):

445781   would be stored at address 781

447883   would be stored at address 883

134552   would be stored at address 552

What will happen when the record with key 631552 is to be stored? This will hash to the same address as 134552 and is called a **synonym**. Synonyms are bound to occur with any hashing algorithm, and two record keys hashing to the same address is referred to as a **collision**.

A simple way of dealing with collisions is to store the item in the next available free space. Thus 134552 would be stored at address 553, assuming this space is unoccupied.

Hash table

A hash table is a collection of items stored in such a way that they can quickly be located. The hash table could be implemented as an array or list of a given size with a number of empty spaces. An empty hash table that can store a maximum of 11 items is shown below, with spaces labelled 0,1, 2,…10.

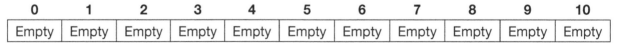

0	1	2	3	4	5	6	7	8	9	10
Empty	Empty	Empty	Empty	Empty	Empty	Empty	Empty	Empty	Empty	Empty

Now assume we wish to store items 78, 55, 34, 19 and 29 in the table using the method described above, using division by 11 and taking the remainder. Collisions are stored in the next available free slot.

First of all, calculate the hash value of each item to be stored.

Item	Hash value
78	1
55	0
34	1
19	8
29	7

Each of these items can now be inserted into their location in the hash table.

0	1	2	3	4	5	6	7	8	9	10
55	78	34	Empty	Empty	Empty	Empty	29	19	Empty	Empty

Q1: Which of the items has caused a collision?

Searching for an item

When searching for an item, these steps are followed:

- apply the hashing algorithm

- examine the resulting cell in the list

- if the item is there, return the item

- if the cell is empty, the item is not in the table

- if there is another item in that spot, keep moving forward until either the item is found or a blank cell is encountered, when it is apparent that the item is not in the table

Other hashing algorithms

To be as efficient as possible, the hashing algorithm needs to be chosen so that it generates the least number of collisions. This will depend to some extent on the distribution of the items to be hashed.

Folding method

There are many other algorithms. The **folding** method divides the item into equal parts, and adds the parts to give the hash value. For example, a phone number 01543 677896 can be divided into groups of two, namely 01, 54, 36, 77, 89, 6. Adding these together, we get 263. If the table has fewer spaces than the maximum possible sum generated by this method, say 100 cells, then the extra steps of dividing by 100 and obtaining the remainder needs to be applied.

Q2: Using the folding method and division by 100, complete the hash table below to show where each number will be stored in a table of 100 spaces. (A sample 123456 is done for you.)

(i) 238464   (ii) 188947   (iii) 276084

Item	"Folded" value	Remainder	Location in hash table
123456	12+34+56=102	2	2
238464			
188947			
276084			

7-40

Hashing a string

A hash function can be created for alphanumeric strings by using the ASCII code for each character. A portion of the ASCII table is shown below:

Character	ASCII value
A	65
B	66
C	67
D	68
E	69
F	70
G	71

To hash the word CAB, we could add up the ASCII values for each letter and, if there are 11 spaces in the hash table, for example, divide by 11 and take the remainder as its hash value.

$67 + 65 + 66 = 198$ Hash value $= 198 \bmod 11 = 0$

so CAB goes in location 0 (assuming that location is empty).

Q3: (i)   Using the above hashing algorithm, find the hash values of the following: BAG, TEA, EAT, GAB. (ASCII code for 'T' = 84)

(i)   What do you notice about the hash values associated with these words?

(iii) Can you suggest a modification of the hashing algorithm that may result in fewer collisions?

7-40

Collision resolution

The fuller the hash table becomes, the more likely it is that there will be collisions, and this needs to be taken into account when designing the hashing algorithm and deciding on the table size. For example, the size of the table could be designed so that when all the items are stored, only 70% of the table's cells are occupied.

Rehashing is the name given to the process of finding an empty slot when a collision has occurred. The rehashing algorithm used above simply looks for the next empty slot. It will loop round to the first cell if the table of the end is reached. A variation on this would be to look at every third cell, for example (the "plus 3" rehash). Alternatively, the hash value could be incremented by 1, 3, 5, 7, … until a free space is found.

Different hashing and rehashing methods will work more efficiently on different data sets – the aim is to minimise collisions.

Uses of hash tables

Hash tables are primarily used for efficient lookup, so that for example an index would typically be organised as a hash table. A hash table could be used to look up, say a person's telephone number given their name, or vice versa. They can also be used to store data such as user codes and encrypted passwords that need to be looked up and verified quickly.

Hash tables are used in the implementation of the data structure called a **dictionary**, which is discussed below.

Dictionaries

A dictionary is an abstract data type consisting of associated pairs of items, where each pair consists of a **key** and a **value**. It is a built-in data structure in Python and Visual Basic, for example. When the user supplies the key, the associated value is returned. Items can easily be amended, added to or removed from the dictionary as required.

In Python, dictionaries are written as comma-delimited pairs in the format **key:value** and enclosed in curly braces. For example:

```
IDs = {342:'Harry', 634:'Jasmine', 885:'Max',571:'Sheila'}
```

Operations on dictionaries

It is possible to implement a dictionary using either a static or a dynamic data structure. The implementation needs to include the following operations:

- Create a new empty dictionary
- Add a new `key:value` pair to the dictionary
- Delete a `key:value` pair from the dictionary
- Amend the value in a `key:value` pair
- Return a value associated with key `k`
- Return `True` or `False` depending on whether key is in the dictionary
- Return the length of the dictionary

An interactive Python session is shown below:

7-40

```
>>> IDs = {342:'Harry', 634:'Jasmine', 885:'Max', 571:'Sheila'}
>>> IDs
{634: 'Jasmine', 571: 'Sheila', 885: 'Max', 342: 'Harry'}
>>> IDs[885]
'Max'
>>> IDs[333] = 'Maria'
>>> IDs
{634: 'Jasmine', 571: 'Sheila', 885: 'Max', 342: 'Harry', 333: 'Maria'}
>>> IDs[885] = 'Maxine'
>>> IDs

{634: 'Jasmine', 571: 'Sheila', 885: 'Maxine', 342: 'Harry', 333:
'Maria'}
>>> del IDs[885]
>>> IDs
{634: 'Jasmine', 571: 'Sheila', 342: 'Harry', 333: 'Maria'}
>>> 634 in IDs
True
>>> len(IDs)
4
```

Note that the pairs are not held in any particular sequence. The key is hashed using a hashing algorithm and placed at the resulting location in a hash table, so that a fast lookup is possible.

Example 1

Suppose we are given a piece of text, and wish to find the number of occurrences of each word. The results will be held in a dictionary. For example, in the text "*one man went to mow, went to mow a meadow, one man and his dog, went to mow a meadow*" the dictionary would start with the key value pairs in the format *{word:frequency}*: {'one':2, 'man':2, 'went':3, 'to':3, …}.

The procedure is basically as follows:

```
Read the text word by word
Check if the word exists in the dictionary
If No, add the word to the dictionary with the value 1
Otherwise, increase the frequency value of the word by 1
```

Note that if the dictionary is implemented as a hash table, as in the Python built-in data structure, the words will not be in alphabetical sequence in the dictionary.

Exercises

1. Student records held by a school are stored in a database which organises the data in files using hashing.

   (a) In the context of storing data in a file, explain what a hash function is. [1]

   (b) The system allows for a maximum of 1000 unique 6-digit integer student IDs in the file holding current student records. Give an example of a hashing function that could be used to find a particular record. Ignore collisions. [2]

2. A bank has a number of safety deposit boxes in which customers can store valuable documents or possessions. The details of which box is rented by a customer with a particular account number are held in a dictionary data structure. Sample entries in the dictionary are:

   {0083456: 'C11', 0154368: 'B74', 1178612: 'B6', 0567123: 'A34'}

   (a) What value will be returned by a lookup operation using the key 1178612? [1]

   (b) The dictionary is implemented using a hash table, using the algorithm

   accountNumber mod 500

   What value is returned by the hashing function when it is applied to account number 0093421? [1]

   (c) What is the maximum number of entries that can be made in the dictionary? [1]

   (d) (i) Explain what is meant by a collision. [1]

   (ii) Give an example of how a collision might occur in this scenario, using sample account numbers. [2]

   (iii) Describe **one** way of dealing with collisions in the hash table. [1]

7-40

Chapter 41 – Graphs

Objectives

- Be aware of a graph as a data structure used to represent complex relationships

- Be familiar with typical uses for graphs

- Be able to explain the terms: graph, weighted graph, vertex/node, edge/arc, undirected graph, directed graph

- Know how an adjacency matrix and an adjacency list may be used to represent a graph

- Be able to compare the use of adjacency matrices and adjacency lists

Definition of a graph

A graph is a set of **vertices** or **nodes** connected by **edges** or **arcs**. The edges may be one-way or two way. In an **undirected graph**, all edges are bidirectional. If the edges in a graph are all one-way, the graph is said to be a **directed graph** or **digraph.**

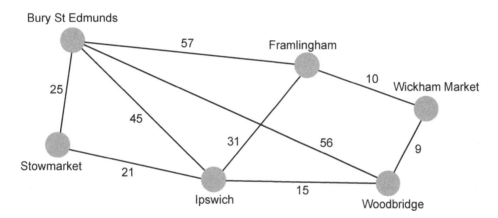

Figure 41.1: An undirected graph with weighted edges

The edges may be **weighted** to show there is a cost to go from one vertex to another as in Figure 41.1. The weights in this example represent distances between towns. A human driver can find their way from one town to another by following a map, but a computer needs to represent the information about distances and connections in a structured, numerical representation.

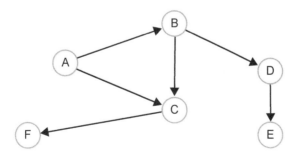

Figure 41.2: A directed, unweighted graph

7-41

Implementing a graph

Two possible implementations of a graph are the **adjacency matrix** and the **adjacency list**.

The adjacency matrix

A two-dimensional array can be used to store information about a directed or undirected graph. Each of the rows and columns represents a node, and a value stored in the cell at the intersection of row i, column j indicates that there is an edge connecting node i and node j.

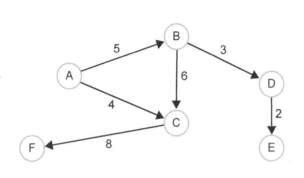

	A	B	C	D	E	F
A		5	4			
B			6	3		
C						8
D					2	
E						
F						

In the case of an **undirected graph**, the adjacency matrix will be symmetric, with the same entry in row 0 column 1 as in row 1 column 0, for example.

An unweighted graph may be represented with 1s instead of weights, in the relevant cells.

7-41

Q1: Draw an adjacency matrix to represent the weighted graph shown in Figure 41.1.

Advantages and disadvantages of the adjacency matrix

An adjacency matrix is very convenient to work with, and adding an edge or testing for the presence of an edge is very simple and quick. However, a sparse graph with many nodes but not many edges will leave most of the cells empty, and the larger the graph, the more memory space will be wasted. Another consideration is that using a static two-dimensional array, it is harder to add or delete nodes.

The adjacency list

An adjacency list is a more space-efficient way to implement a sparsely connected graph. A list of all the nodes is created, and each node points to a list of all the adjacent nodes to which it is directly linked. The adjacency list can be implemented as a list of dictionaries, with the key in each dictionary being the node and the value, the edge weight.

The graph above would be represented as follows:

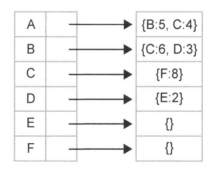

A	→	{B:5, C:4}
B	→	{C:6, D:3}
C	→	{F:8}
D	→	{E:2}
E	→	{}
F	→	{}

The unweighted graph in Figure 41.2 would be represented as shown below, with the adjacency list containing lists of nodes adjacent to each node. A dictionary data structure is not required here as there are no edge weights.

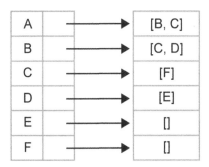

The advantage of this implementation is that is uses much less memory to represent a sparsely connected graph.

> **Q2:** Draw an adjacency list to represent the unweighted graph shown in Figure 41.2, but assuming this time that it is undirected.

Applications of graphs

Graphs may be used to represent, for example:

- computer networks, with nodes representing computers and weighted edges representing the bandwidth between them
- roads between towns, with edge weights representing distances, rail fares or journey times
- tasks in a project, some of which have to be completed before others
- states in a finite state machine
- web pages and links

Google's PageRank algorithm

In the 1990s two postgraduate Computer Science students called Larry Page and Sergey Brin met at Stanford University. Brin was working on data mining systems and Page was working on a system to rank the importance of a research paper according to how often it was cited in other papers.

The pair realised that this concept could be used to build a far superior search engine to the existing ones, and they started to work on a new Search Engine for the Web. The problem they set themselves was how to rank the thousands or even millions of web pages that had a reference to the search term typed in by a user. To make a search engine useful, the most reliable and relevant pages need to appear first in the list of links.

Until that point, pages had generally been ranked simply by the number of times the search term appeared on the page. Page's and Brin's insight was to realise that the usefulness and therefore the **rank** of a given page, say Page X, can be determined by how many visits to Page X result from other web pages containing links to the page. Taking this further, links from a Page Y that itself has a high rank are more significant than those from pages which have themselves only had a few visits. The importance or authority of a page is also taken into account so that a link from a .gov page or a page belonging to the BBC site, for example, may be given a higher PageRank rating.

7-41

An initial version of Google was launched in August 1996 from Stanford University's website. By mid-1998 they had 10,000 searches a day, and realised the potential of their invention.

They represented the Web as a directed graph of pages, using an algorithm to calculate the PageRank (named after Larry Page) of each page. Every web page is a node and any hyperlinks on the page are edges, with the edge weightings dependent on the PageRank algorithm.

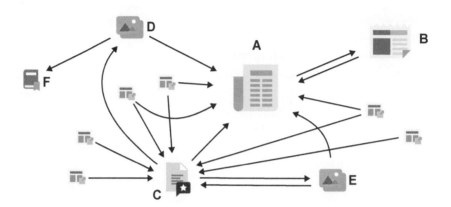

*Using PageRank, **B** has a higher page rank than **C** because it is a more authoritative source.*

By 2015, Google was processing 40,000 search queries every second, worldwide. David Vise, the author of The Google Story noted that "Not since Gutenberg* … has any new invention empowered individuals, and transformed access to information, as profoundly as Google."

(*Gutenberg invented the printing press in the fifteenth century)

Exercises

1. The figure below shows an adjacency matrix representation of a directed graph (digraph).

<table>
<tr><td></td><td></td><td colspan="5">To</td></tr>
<tr><td></td><td></td><td>A</td><td>B</td><td>C</td><td>D</td><td>E</td></tr>
<tr><td rowspan="5">From</td><td>A</td><td>0</td><td>5</td><td>3</td><td>10</td><td>0</td></tr>
<tr><td>B</td><td>0</td><td>0</td><td>1</td><td>8</td><td>0</td></tr>
<tr><td>C</td><td>0</td><td>0</td><td>0</td><td>7</td><td>6</td></tr>
<tr><td>D</td><td>0</td><td>0</td><td>0</td><td>0</td><td>4</td></tr>
<tr><td>E</td><td>0</td><td>0</td><td>0</td><td>0</td><td>0</td></tr>
</table>

(a) Draw a diagram of the directed graph, showing edge weights. [3]

(b) Draw an adjacency list representing this graph. [3]

(c) Give **one** advantage of using an adjacency matrix to represent a graph, and **one** advantage of using an adjacency list. Explain the circumstances in which each is more appropriate. [3]

2. Graph algorithms are used with GPS navigation systems, social networking sites, computer networks, computer games, exam timetabling, matching problems and many other applications.

Describe **two** practical applications of graphs. [6]

Chapter 42 – Trees

Objectives

- Know that a tree is a connected, undirected graph with no cycles
- Know that a binary tree is a rooted tree in which each node has at most two children
- Be familiar with typical uses for rooted trees

Concept of a tree

Trees are a very common data structure in many areas of computer science and other contexts. A family tree is an example of a tree, and a folder structure where a root directory has many folders and sub-folders is another example. Like a tree in nature, a **rooted tree** has a root, branches and leaves, the difference being that a rooted tree in computer science has its root at the top and its leaves at the bottom.

Typical uses for rooted trees include:

- manipulating hierarchical data, such as folder structures or moves in a game
- making information easy to search (see binary tree search below)
- manipulating sorted lists of data

The uses of various tree-traversal algorithms are covered in Section 8, Chapter 44.

Generations of a family may be thought of as having a tree structure:

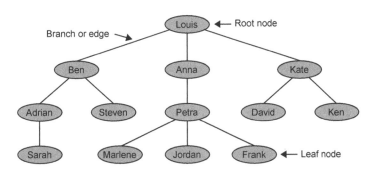

The tree shown above has a **root node**, and is therefore defined as a **rooted tree**. Here are some terms used in connection with rooted trees:

Node: The nodes contain the tree data

Edge: An edge connects two nodes. Every node except the root is connected by exactly one edge from another node in the level above it

Root: This is the only node that has no incoming edges

Child: The set of nodes that have incoming edges from the same node

Parent: A node is a parent of all the nodes it connects to with outgoing edges

Subtree: The set of nodes and edges comprised of a parent and all descendants of the parent. A subtree may also be a leaf

Leaf node: A node that has no children

Q1: Identify the left subtree of the root, the parent of Frank and the children of Kate. How many parent nodes are there in the tree? How many child nodes?

7-42

Note that a rooted tree is a special case of a **connected graph**. A node can only be connected to one parent node, and to its children. It is described as having has no **cycles** because there can be no connection between children, or between branches, for example from Ben to Anna or Petra to Kate.

A more general definition of a tree

A tree is a connected, undirected graph with no cycles. "Connected" implies that it is always possible to find a path from a node to any other node, by backtracking if necessary. "No cycles" means that it is not possible to find a path in the tree which returns to the start node without traversing an edge twice. Note that a tree does not have to have a root.

Q2: Using the above definition of a tree, which of the following diagrams represents a tree? If any of them does not represent a tree, explain why.

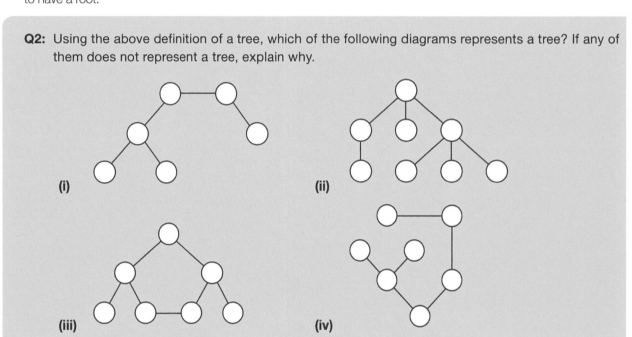

(i)

(ii)

(iii)

(iv)

A binary search tree

A **binary tree** is a rooted tree in which each node has a maximum of two children. A **binary search tree** holds items in such a way that the tree can be searched quickly and easily for a particular item, new items can be easily added, and the whole tree can be printed out in sequence. A binary search tree is a typical use of a rooted tree.

Constructing a binary search tree

Suppose the following list of numbers is to be inserted into a binary tree, in the order given, in such a way that the tree can be quickly searched.

17, 8, 4, 12, 22, 19, 14, 5, 30, 25

The tree is constructed using the following algorithm:

Place the first item at the root. Then for each item in the list, visit the root, which becomes the current node, and branch left if the item is less than the value at the current node, and right if the item is greater than the value at the current node. Continue down the branch, applying the rule at each node visited, until a leaf node is reached. The item is then placed to the left or right of this node, depending on whether it is less than or greater than the value at that node.

Following this algorithm, 17 is placed at the root. 8 is less than 17, so is placed at a new node to the left of the root.

4 is less than 17, so we branch left at the root, branch left at 8, and place it to the left.

12 is less than 17, so we branch left at the root, branch right at 8, and place it to the right.

The final tree looks like this:

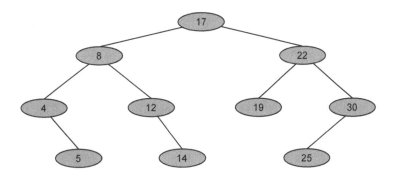

To search the tree for the number 19, for example, we follow the same steps.

19 is greater than 17, so branch right.

19 is less than 22, so branch left. There it is!

Q3: (a) Which nodes will be visited when searching for the number 14?

(b) Which nodes will be visited when searching for the number 21, which is not in the tree?

(c) Where will new nodes 10 and 20 be inserted?

Traversing a binary tree

There are three ways of traversing a tree:

- Pre-order traversal
- In-order traversal
- Post-order traversal

The names refer to whether the root of each sub-tree is visited before, between or after both branches have been traversed.

Pre-order traversal

Draw an outline around the tree structure, starting to the left of the root. As you pass to the left of a node (where the red dot is marked), output the data in that node.

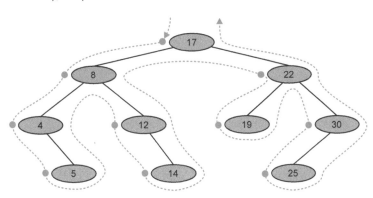

The nodes will be visited in the sequence 17, 8, 4, 5, 12, 14, 22, 19, 30, 25

A pre-order traversal may be used to produce prefix notation, used in functional programming languages. A simple illustration would be a function statement, `x = sum a,b` rather than `x = a + b`, in which the operation comes before the operands rather than between them, as in infix notation.

In-order traversal

Draw an outline around the tree structure, starting to the left of the root. As you pass underneath a node (where the red dot is marked), output the data in that node.

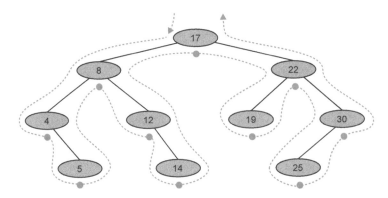

The nodes will be visited in the sequence 4, 5, 8, 12, 14, 17, 19, 22, 25, 30.

The in-order traversal visits the nodes in sequential order.

Q4: Construct a binary search tree to hold the names Mark, Stephanie, Chigozie, Paul, Anne, Hanna, Luke, David, Vincent, Tom. List the names, in the order they would be checked, to find David.

Q5: List the names in the order they would be output when an in-order traversal is performed.

Post-order traversal

Draw an outline around the tree structure, starting to the left of the root. As you pass to the right of a node (where the red dot is marked), output the data in that node.

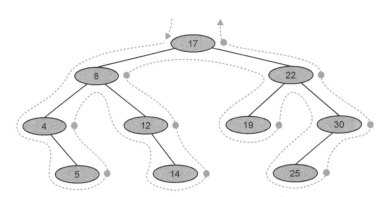

The nodes will be visited in the sequence 5, 4, 14, 12, 8, 10, 25, 30, 22, 17.

Post-order traversal is used in program compilation to produce **Reverse Polish Notation** (Chapter 55).

Algorithms for implementing a binary tree and each of these traversals will be covered in Chapter 44.

7-42

Implementation of a binary search tree

A binary search tree can be implemented using an array of records, with each node consisting of:

- left pointer
- data item
- right pointer

Alternatively, it could be held in a two-dimensional list, or three separate lists or arrays, one for each of the pointers and one for the data items.

The numbers 17, 8, 4, 12, 22, 19, 14, 5, 30, 25 used to construct the tree above could be held as follows:

	left	data	right
tree[0]	1	17	4
tree[1]	2	8	3
tree[2]	-1	4	7
tree[3]	-1	12	6
tree[4]	5	22	8
tree[5]	-1	19	-1
tree[6]	-1	14	-1
tree[7]	-1	5	-1
tree[8]	9	30	3
tree[9]	-1	25	-1

7-42

For example, the left pointer in tree[0] points to tree[1] and the right pointer points to tree[4]. The value -1 is a 'rogue value' which indicates that there is no child on the relevant side (left or right).

Q6: Show how the search tree below could be implemented in an array with left and right pointers.

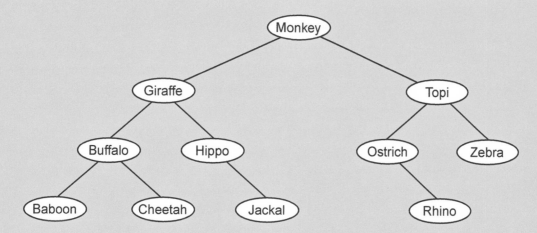

Names were inserted in the tree in the following order: Monkey, Topi, Ostrich, Giraffe, Hippo, Zebra, Buffalo, Cheetah, Rhino, Baboon, Jackal

Exercises

1. Figure 1 shows an adjacency matrix representation of a directed graph (digraph).

Figure 1

	To				
	1	**2**	**3**	**4**	**5**
1	0	1	0	1	0
2	0	0	1	1	0
3	0	0	0	0	0
4	0	0	0	0	1
5	0	1	0	0	0

(*From* labels the rows)

(a) Complete this unfinished diagram of the directed graph. [2]

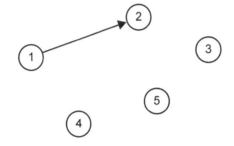

(b) Directed graphs can also be represented by an adjacency list.

Explain under what circumstances an adjacency matrix is the most appropriate method to represent a directed graph, and under what circumstances an adjacency list is more appropriate. [2]

(c) A tree is a particular type of graph.

What properties must a graph have for it to be a tree? [2]

(d) Data may be stored as a binary tree.

Show how the following data may be stored as a binary tree for subsequent processing in alphabetic order by drawing the tree. Assume that the first item is the root of the tree and the rest of the data items are inserted into the tree in the order given.

Data items: Jack, Bramble, Snowy, Butter, Squeak, Bear, Pip [3]

(e) A binary tree such as the one created in part (d) could be represented using one array of records or, alternatively, using three one dimensional arrays.

Describe how the data in the array(s) could be structured for one of these two possible methods of representation. [3]

AQA Comp 3 Qu 7 2010

7-42

Chapter 43 – Vectors

Objectives

- Be familiar with the concept of a vector and notations for specifying a vector as a list of numbers, as a function or as a geometric point in space

- Represent a vector using a list, dictionary or array data structure

- Perform operations on vectors: addition, scalar vector multiplication, convex combination, dot or scalar product

- Describe applications of dot product of two vectors

Vector notation

A **vector** can be represented as:

- a list of numbers

- a function

- a way of representing a geometric point in space

There are several different notations for specifying a given vector.

1. A list of numbers may be written as [2.0, 3.14159, -1.0, 2.71828].

2. A 4-vector over $\mathbb{R}$ such as [2.0, 3.14159, -1.0, 2.71828] may be written as $\mathbb{R}^4$

3. A vector may be interpreted as a function, $f : S \mapsto \mathbb{R}$ where S is the set {0, 1, 2, 3} and $\mathbb{R}$ the set of real numbers

    For example

    $0 \mapsto 2.0$

    $1 \mapsto 3.14159$

    $2 \mapsto 1.0$

    $3 \mapsto 2.71828$ where $\mapsto$ means "maps to"

    Note that all the entries must be drawn from the same field, e.g. $\mathbb{R}$.

Vectors in up to 3 dimensions, ie up to $\mathbb{R}^3$ can also be conveniently represented geometrically, and this will be explained later in the chapter.

Implementation of vectors in a programming language

In Python, for example, a vector may be represented as a list: [2.0, 3.14159, -1.0, 2.71828]

In a different language, it could be represented in a one-dimensional array.

The 4-vector example could be represented as a dictionary: {0:2.0, 1:3.14159, 2: -1.0, 3: 2.71828}

Vectors in computer science

Many applications in Computing involve processing spatial information. For example:

- a computer controlling a robot arm needs to keep track of its current coordinates, and work out how to move it to its next location

- computer games and simulations need to work out how objects moving in 3-D space can be represented on the screen; for example, how does a ball move when it is struck by a golf club?

- on-board computers in fly-by-wire aircraft need to take into account wind speed and direction when setting and holding a course in three dimensions.

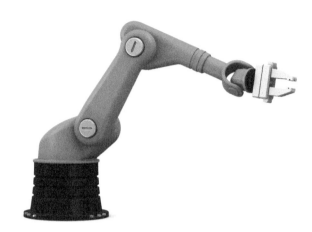

In order to perform these tasks, the computer must represent spatial information and movement in a numerical way. In mathematics, **vectors** and **matrices** are used to do this, and these concepts are crucial for any computer application which involves spatial movement.

Vectors in mathematics

In mathematics, a very common use of vectors is as a numerical way of describing and processing spatial information such as **position**, **velocity**, **acceleration** or **force**.

Velocity may be represented by a vector showing both speed and direction. This can be shown graphically by an arrow with its tail at the origin and its head at coordinates (x,y). Speed is represented by length **a**, and direction by the angle between **A** and the x-axis.

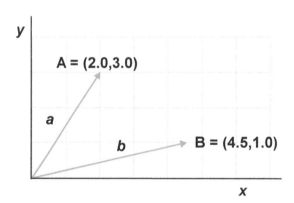

The graphical representation shows how a vector consisting of just two numbers can represent both **magnitude** and **direction**.

Adding and subtracting vectors

Vectors may be added by adding the x and y coordinates separately:

C = A + B = (2.0 + 4.5, 3.0 + 1.0) = (6.5, 4.0)

The resultant vector can be represented graphically by moving the vector **b** so that it joins on to the end of **a**. The resulting vector **c** will represent the new magnitude and direction. Physically, you can imagine an aeroplane flying at speed **b**, with a wind **a** blowing at an angle to the direction of flight: the aeroplane will actually travel with the combined speed and direction shown by the vector **c** in the graph below.

7-43

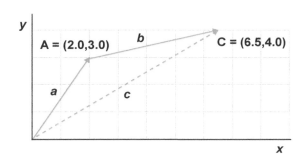

Q1: How can we calculate the lengths of the lines marked **a** and **c**?

We can also subtract the vector **a** from the vector **b**, to get a vector **d** = (2.5, -2.0). This might represent a wind **a** blowing in the opposite direction.

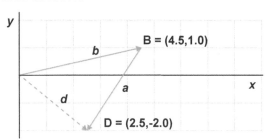

Example

A vector **Current** represents the speed (in km/hr) and direction of a current. A swimmer, who swims at 8km/hr, has to swim to a buoy at B, and we need to find the direction he should swim in (marked Swimmer).

7-43

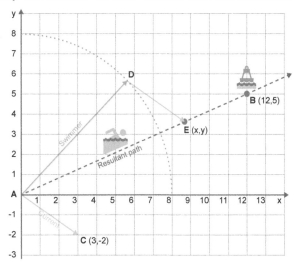

The vector **Swimmer** must lie on the arc of radius 8 shown in red, since any point on this arc represents the distance the swimmer will travel in one hour. To find the direction he must swim in, we need to transpose the current vector so that it its tail is on the arc and its head on the desired resultant path. If he keeps swimming in direction AD he will eventually reach the buoy at B.

```
swimmer = resultant path - current
        = (x,y) - (3,-2)
        = (x-3, y+2)
```

Scaling vectors

A vector can be scaled by multiplying it by a value. In the figure below, B = 3 * A.

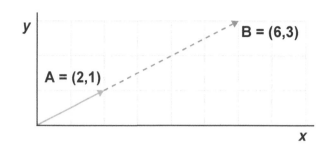

Convex combination of two vectors

A **convex combination of vectors** is an expression of the form

$\alpha u + \beta v$ where $\alpha + \beta = 1$ and $\alpha,\ \beta \geq 0$

e.g.   0.7 *(5.0, 3.0) + 0.3 * (4.0 ,2.0) = (3.5, 2.1) + (1.2, 0.6) = (4.7, 2.7)

In the diagram below, if A and B represent two vectors, any vector C represented by (αA + βB) must lie within the shaded area between A and B.

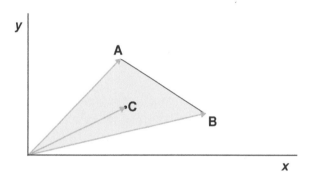

7-43

> **Q2:** If two vectors P and Q are defined as P = (0,4) and Q = (6,0), draw the vector space represented by
>
> R = αP + βQ   where $\alpha + \beta = 1$ and $\alpha,\ \beta \geq 0$
>
> Mark on the diagram the position of vector R = 0.75P + 0.25Q

Dot product of two vectors

To find the **dot product** (sometimes called the **scalar product**) of two vectors, each component of the first vector is multiplied by the corresponding component of the second vector, and the products are added together.

The dot product of two vectors u and v where $u = [u_1, ..., u_n]$ and $v = [v_1, ..., v_n]$ is

    $u \bullet v = u_1 v_1 + u_2 v_2 + ... + u_n v_n$

    Thus [2, 3, 4] $\bullet$ [5, 2, 1] = 10 + 6 + 4 = 20

Notice that the result of the dot product is a **number**, not a vector, and it can be used as a way to compare two vectors.

The Galois field of two elements: GF(2)

There is another, more general, interpretation of a vector as a mapping from one set of values to another. In mathematics, the **Galois field** of two elements is referred to as GF(2). The two elements are called 0 and 1. The addition and multiplication operations correspond to the logical operations XOR and AND, the tables for which are shown below.

+	0	1
0	0	1
1	1	0

XOR ($\oplus$) table: e.g. 1 XOR 1 = 0

*	0	1
0	0	0
1	0	1

AND ($\bullet$) table: e.g. 1 AND 1 = 1

From the first table, therefore, $1 \oplus 1 = 0$ (replacing XOR with the symbol $\oplus$)

Given two vectors u and v over GF(2), defined as u = [1, 1, 1, 1] and v = [1, 0, 1, 1]

the dot product u $\bullet$ v is defined as

$$u \bullet v = 1 \bullet 1 \oplus 1 \bullet 0 \oplus 1 \bullet 1 \oplus 1 \bullet 1$$

Interpreting these terms in GF(2), this is equivalent to

$$u \bullet v = (1 \text{ AND } 1) \text{ XOR } (1 \text{ AND } 0) \text{ XOR } (1 \text{ AND } 1) \text{ XOR } (1 \text{ AND } 1)$$

$$= 1 \text{ XOR } 0 \text{ XOR } 1 \text{ XOR } 1$$

$$= 1$$

7-43

Application as a parity bit checker

This use of vectors can be interpreted as a parity bit calculator or checker as, if the vector u is filled with 1s and the vector v contains the bit pattern for which a parity bit is required (in this example 1011), then the output of u $\bullet$ v can be interpreted either as the parity bit that needs to be added to the bit pattern to achieve even parity (1011 → 1011**1**) or as an indicator of whether the bit pattern as it stands has even or odd parity (0 = has even parity, 1 = has odd parity).

Exercises

1. Two vectors A and B are defined as A = (1, 3) and B = (10, 4). Calculate:

(a) A + B   [1]

(b) A • B   [1]

(c) 3 * A   [1]

2. (a) A and B are two vectors implemented as lists. Trace through the following pseudocode and state what is printed. What does the program calculate?   [3]

```
SUB calcX(A,B)
    calcAB ← 0
    for i ← 0 TO len(A) - 1
        calcAB ← calcAB + (A[i] + B[i])
    END FOR
    RETURN calcAB
ENDSUB

#main
A ← [3,4]
B ← [2,1]
x ← calc(A,B)
OUTPUT x
```

(b) (i) What are the coordinates (x, y) of the normalised vector B in the following diagram?

(Note: A normalised vector always has length 1.)

[2]

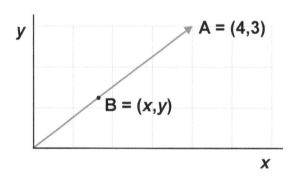

(ii) Write a pseudocode subroutine `normalise(A)` to normalise a vector A(x, y).   [4]

3. Vectors may be interpreted in different ways. In the Galois field GF(2), the operation of addition corresponds to logical XOR and the operation of multiplication corresponds to logical AND.

(a) Using this interpretation, calculate the dot product of two vectors (1, 0, 0, 1) and (1, 1, 1, 1). Show how you arrive at this result.   [3]

(b) It is required to use this technique to calculate the parity bit for a 7-digit bit pattern. Explain, using the bit pattern 1010110 as an example, how the dot product of two vectors in GF(2) may be used to give the value of the 8th bit (the parity bit) that needs to be added to achieve even parity.   [3]

7-43

Section 8

Algorithms

In this section:

8

Chapter 44 – Recursive algorithms

Objectives

- Be familiar with the use of recursive techniques in programming languages

- Be able to solve simple problems using recursion

- Be able to trace recursive tree-traversal algorithms: pre-order, post-order, in-order

- Be able to describe uses of tree-traversal algorithms

Definition of a recursive subroutine

A subroutine is **recursive** if it is defined in terms of itself. The process of executing the subroutine is called **recursion**.

A recursive routine has three essential characteristics:

- A stopping condition or **base case** must be included which when met means that the routine will not call itself and will start to 'unwind'

- For input values other than the stopping condition, the routine must call itself

- The stopping condition must be reached after a finite number of calls

Recursion is a useful technique for the programmer when the algorithm itself is essentially recursive.

Example

A simple example of a recursive routine is the calculation of a factorial, where **n!** (read as **factorial n**) is defined as follows:

If n = 0 then n! = 1

otherwise n! = n x (n-1) x (n-2) ... x 3 x 2 x 1

Thus for example 5! = 5 x 4 x 3 x 2 x 1

If we were calculating this manually, we probably calculate 5 x 4 =20, then multiply 20 by 3 and so on. The calculation could be written as

5! = ((((5 x 4) x 3) x 2) x 1) = (((20 x 3) x 2) x 1) = ((60 x 2) x 1) = 120 x 1 = 120

This is essentially how recursion works. In pseudocode, it can be written like this:

```
SUB calcFactorial(n)
    IF n = 0 THEN
        factorial ← 1
    ELSE
        factorial ← n * calcFactorial(n-1)
        OUTPUT factorial      #LINE A
    ENDIF
    RETURN factorial
ENDSUB
```

Nothing will be printed until the routine has stopped calling itself. As soon as the stopping condition is reached, in this case n = 0, the variable `factorial` is set equal to 1, the return statement at the end of the subroutine is reached and control is passed back (for the first time, but not the last) to the next statement after the last call to `calcFactorial`, which is the OUTPUT statement marked LINE A.

Use of the call stack

In Chapter 39 the use of the **call stack** was discussed. Each time a subroutine is called, the return address, parameters and local variables used in the subroutine are held in a **stack frame** in the call stack. The following representations of the current state of the stack each time a recursive call is made, and the subsequent "unwinding" is shown when the routine is called from the main program.

Consider the following example:

```
1. SUB printList(num)
2.    num ← num - 1
3.    IF num > 1 THEN printList(num)
4.    OUTPUT "At B, num = ", num      #Line B
5. ENDSUB
6. #main program
7. x ← 4
8. printList(x)
9. OUTPUT "At A, x =", x          #Line A
```

Return addresses, parameters and local variables (not used here) are put on the stack each time a subroutine is called, and popped from the stack each time the end of a subroutine is reached. At Line 8, for example, Line 9 (referred to here as Line A) is the first return address to be put on the stack with the parameter 4 when printlist(x) is called from the main program, with the parameter 4.

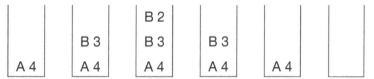

The output from the program is:

At B, num = 1   (printed at Line B)

At B, num = 2   (printed at Line B)

At B, num = 3   (printed at Line B)

At A, x = 4   (printed at Line A)

Tree traversal algorithms

In the previous chapter, three tree traversal algorithms were described: in-order, pre-order and post-order. The pseudocode algorithm for each of these traversals is recursive.

The algorithm for an in-order traversal is

```
traverse the left subtree
visit the root node
traverse the right subtree
```

8-44

Example of in-order traversal

An algebraic expression is represented by the following binary tree. It could be represented in memory as, for example, three 1-dimensional arrays or as a list with each list element holding the data and left and right pointers to the left and right subtrees. The value of the root node is stored as the first element of the list.

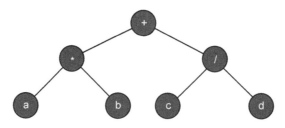

Figure 1

Suppose this data is held as shown below:

	left	data	right
tree[0]	1	+	2
tree[1]	3	*	4
tree[2]	5	/	6
tree[3]	-1	a	-1
tree[4]	-1	b	-1
tree[5]	-1	c	-1
tree[6]	-1	d	-1

In pseudocode:

```
SUB inorderTraverse(p)
   IF tree[p].left <> -1 THEN
      inorderTraverse(tree[p].left)
   ENDIF
   OUTPUT (tree[p].data)
   IF tree[p].right <> -1 THEN
      inorderTraverse(tree[p].right)
   ENDIF
ENDSUB
```

The routine is called with a statement `inorderTraverse(0)`

Tracing through the algorithm, the nodes are output in the order **a * b + c / d**.

Use of in-order traversal algorithm

An in-order traversal may be used to output the values held in the nodes in alphabetic or numerical sequence. An example is given in Chapter 42.

Algorithm for post-order traversal

The algorithm for a post-order traversal is

```
traverse the left subtree
traverse the right subtree
visit the root node
```

8-44

In pseudocode:

```
SUB postorderTraverse(p)
   IF tree[p].left <> -1 THEN
      postorderTraverse(tree[p].left)
   ENDIF
   IF tree[p].right <> -1 THEN
      postorderTraverse(tree[p].right)
   ENDIF
   OUTPUT (tree[p].data)
ENDSUB
```

**Bury College
Millennium LRC**

The nodes are output in the sequence **a b * c d / +**. This is the sequence in which algebraic expressions are written using **Reverse Polish Notation**, which is covered in Chapter 55.

Example of pre-order traversal

Suppose we have a tree which represents the structure of a formal report for a project. It could be structured as follows:

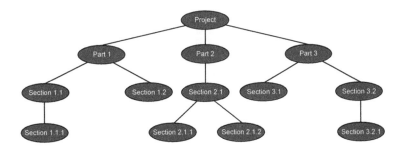

8-44

Traversing this tree using a pre-order traversal, the whole project will be read in sequence. We first visit the root, then the root of the left subtree, and so on until we reach a leaf node. Then we back up as far as a node which has a right subtree.

The algorithm for a pre-order traversal is

```
visit the root node
traverse the left subtree
traverse the right subtree

SUB preorderTraverse(p)
   OUTPUT (tree[p].value)
   IF tree[p].left <> -1 THEN
      preorderTraverse(tree[p].left)
   ENDIF
   IF tree[p].right <> -1 THEN
      preorderTraverse(tree[p].right)
   ENDIF
ENDSUB
```

The nodes are output in the sequence **Project**, **Part 1**, **Section 1.1**, **Section 1.1.1**, **Section 1.2**, **Part 2**, etc.

A pre-order traversal may be used for copying a tree, and for producing a prefix expression from an expression tree such as the one shown in Figure 1. For example, **x + y** in prefix notation is **+ x y**. Prefix is used in some compilers and calculators.

Exercises

1. (a) Explain briefly the main features of a recursive procedure from the programmer's point of view. What is required from the system in order to enable recursion to be used? [3]

(b) The following recursive subroutine carries out a list operation.

```
SUB listProcess(numList)
   IF length(numlist) > 0 THEN
      Remove first element of numlist and store in first
      listProcess (numList)
      append first to end of numList
   ENDIF
   RETURN numList
ENDSUB
```

(i) Complete the following trace table if the list numbers is defined in the main program as

numbers ← [3,5,10,2]

and the subroutine is called with the statement

new ← listProcess(numbers)

length (numlist)	numlist				first	new
	0	1	2	3		
4	3	5	10	2	3	

[6]

(ii) Explain what the subroutine does. [1]

2. The routine stars(n) is called from the main program with the statement stars(4).

```
1. SUB stars(n)
2.    IF n = 1 THEN
3.       RETURN "*"
4.    ELSE
5.       RETURN stars(n-1) + "*"
6.    ENDIF
7. ENDSUB

   #main program
8. line ← stars(4)
9. OUTPUT line
```

(a) How many times is the subroutine stars called? Explain your answer. [4]

(b) What is printed by the final line of the program (line 9)? [1]

(c) What will be printed at line 9 if line 5 is replaced with the following statement?

```
RETURN stars(n-1) + str(n)
```

[1]

Chapter 45 – Big-O notation

Objectives

- Be familiar with the concept of a function as a mapping from one set of values to another
- Be familiar with the concept of linear, polynomial, exponential and logarithmic functions
- Be familiar with the notion of permutation of a set of objects or values
- Be familiar with the Big-O notation to express time complexity
- Be able to derive the time complexity of an algorithm

Comparing algorithms

Algorithms may be compared on how much time they need to solve a particular problem. This is referred to as the **time complexity** of the algorithm. The goal is to design algorithms which will run quickly while taking up the minimal amount of resources such as memory.

In order to compare the efficiency of different algorithms in terms of execution time, we need to quantify the number of basic operations or steps that the algorithm will need, in terms of the number of items to be processed.

For example, consider these two algorithms, which both calculate the sum of the first n integers.

```
SUB sumIntegersMethod1(n)
   sum ← 0
   FOR i ← 1 TO n
      sum ← sum + n
   ENDFOR
   RETURN sum
ENDSUB
```

The second algorithm computes the same sum using a different algorithm:

```
SUB sumIntegersMethod2(n)
   sum ← n * (n+1)/2
   RETURN sum
ENDSUB
```

Q1: Which algorithm is more efficient? Why?

The first algorithm performs one operation (sum ← 0) outside the loop and n operations inside the FOR loop, a total of n + 1 operations. As n increases, the extra operation to initialise sum is insignificant, and the larger the value of n, the more inefficient this algorithm is. Its **order of magnitude** or **time complexity** is basically n. The second algorithm, on the other hand, takes the same amount of time whatever the value of n. Its time complexity is a constant.

We will return to this idea later in the Chapter, but first, we need to look at some of the maths involved in calculating the time complexity of different algorithms.

Introduction to functions

The order of magnitude, or time complexity of an algorithm can be expressed as a **function** of its size.

A function maps one set of values onto another.

INPUT x

FUNCTION f:

OUTPUT f(x)

A linear function

A linear function is expressed in general terms as **f(x) = ax + c**

Values of the function $f(x) = 3x + 4$ are shown below for $x = 1, 10, 100, 10,000$

x	3x	4	y = f(x)
1	3	4	7
10	30	4	34
100	300	4	304
10,000	30,000	4	30,004

Notice that the constant term has proportionally less and less effect on the value of the function as the value of x increases. The only term that is significant is 3x, and f(x) increases in a straight line as x increases.

A polynomial function

A polynomial expression is expressed as **f(x) = ax^m + bx + c**

Values of the function $f(x) = 2x^2 + 10x + 50$ are shown below for $x = 1, 10, 100, 10,000$

x	x²	2x²	10x	50	y = f(x)
1	1	2	10	50	62
10	100	200	100	50	350
100	10,000	20,000	1,000	50	21,050
10,000	100,000,000	200,000,000	100,000	50	200,100,050

The values of b and c have a smaller and smaller effect on the answer as x increases, compared with the value of a. The only term that really matters is the term in x^2, if we are approximating the value of the function for a large value of x.

An exponential function

An exponential function takes the form **f(x) = ab^x**. This function grows very large, very quickly!

Q2: What is the value of $f(x) = 2^x$ when $x = 1$? When $x = 10$? When $x = 100$?

8-45

A logarithmic function

A logarithmic function takes the form $f(x) = a \log_n x$

"The logarithm of a number is the power that the base must be raised to make it equal to the number."

Values of the function $f(x) = \log_2 x$ are shown below for x = 1, 8, 1,024, 1,048,576.

x	$y = \log_2 x$
1	0
8 (2^3)	3
1024 (2^{10})	10
1,048,576 (2^{20})	20

Permutations

The permutation of a set of objects is the number of ways of arranging the objects. For example, if you have 3 objects A, B and C you can choose any of A, B or C to be the first object. You then have two choices for the second object, making 3 x 2 = 6 different ways of arranging the first two objects, and then just one way of placing the third object. The six permutations are ABC, ACB, BAC, BCA, CAB, CBA.

Q3: How many permutations are there of four objects? How many ways are there of arranging six students in a line?

The formula for calculating the number of permutations of four objects is 4 x 3 x 2 x 1, written 4! and spoken as "four factorial". (Note that 10! = 3.6 million… so don't try getting 10 students to line up in all possible ways!)

8-45

Big-O notation

Now that we have got all the maths out of the way and hopefully understood, we can study the so-called **Big-O notation** which is used to express the **time complexity**, or performance, of an algorithm. ('O' stands for 'Order'.)

The best way to understand this notation is to look at some examples.

O(1) (Constant time)

O(1) describes an algorithm that takes **constant time** (the same amount of time) to execute regardless of the size of the input data set.

Suppose array a has n items. The statement

```
length ← len(a)
```

will take the same amount of time to execute however many items are held in the array.

O(n) (linear time)

O(n) describes an algorithm whose performance will grow in **linear time**, in direct proportion to the size of the data set. For example, a linear search of an array of 1000 unsorted items will take 1000 times longer than searching an array of 1 item.

O(n²) (Polynomial time)

O(n²) describes an algorithm whose performance is directly proportional to the square of the size of the data set. A program with two nested loops each performed n times will typically have an order of time complexity O(n²). The running time of the algorithm grows in **polynomial time**.

O(2ⁿ) (Exponential time)

O(2ⁿ) describes an algorithm where the time taken to execute will double with every additional item added to the data set. The execution time grows in **exponential time** and quickly becomes very large.

O(log n) (Logarithmic time)

The time taken to execute an algorithm of order O(log n) (**logarithmic time**) will grow very slowly as the size of the data set increases. A **binary search** is a good example of an algorithm of time complexity O(log n). Doubling the size of the data set has very little effect on the time the algorithm takes to complete. (Note that in Big-O notation the base of the logarithm, 2 in this case, is not specified because it is irrelevant to the time complexity, being a constant factor.)

O(n!) (Exponential time)

The time taken to execute an algorithm of order O(n!) will grow very quickly, faster than O(2ⁿ). Suppose that the problem is to find all the permutations of n letters. If n=2, there are 2 permutations to find. If n=6, there are 720 permutations – far more than 2ⁿ, which is only 64.

8-45

Q4: A hacker trying to discover a password starts by checking a dictionary containing 170,000 words. What is the maximum number of words he will need to try out?

This procedure fails to find the password. He now needs to try random combinations of the letters in the password. He starts with 6-letter combinations of a-z, A-Z.

Explain why the second procedure will take so much longer than the first.

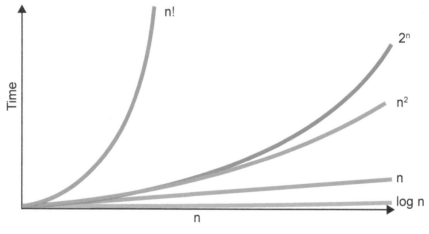

Graphs of log n, n, n², 2ⁿ, n!

Calculating the time complexity of an algorithm

Here are two different algorithms for finding the smallest element in an array called `arrayX` of size n. Assume the index starts at 0.

The first algorithm puts the first value in the array equal to a variable called `minimum`. It then compares each subsequent item in the array to the first item, and if it is smaller, replaces minimum with the new lowest value.

```
minimum ← arrayX[0]
FOR k ← 0 TO n - 1
    IF arrayX[k] < minimum THEN
        minimum ← arrayX[k]
    ENDIF
ENDFOR
```

To calculate the time complexity of the algorithm in Big-O notation, we need to count the number of basic operations relevant to the size of the problem that it performs. The basic operation here is the `IF` statement, and as this is performed n times, the time complexity is O(n).

The second algorithm compares each value in the array to all the other values of the array, and if the current value is less than or equal to all the other values in the array then it is the minimum.

```
FOR k ← 0 to n - 1
    isMinimum ← true
    FOR j ← 0 to n - 1
        IF arrayX[k] > arrayX[j] THEN
            isMinimum ← false
        ENDIF
    ENDFOR
    IF (isMinimum) THEN
        minimum ← arrayX[k]
    ENDIF
ENDFOR
```

To calculate the time complexity of this algorithm, we count the number of basic operations it performs.

There are two basic operations in the outer loop, (`isMinimum ← true` and the final `IF` statement) which are each performed n times. The inner loop has one basic operations performed n^2 times.

This gives us a time complexity of $2n + n^2$, but as discussed earlier, the only significant term is the one in n^2. The time complexity is therefore O(n^2).

8-45

> **Q5:** What is the time complexity of each of the two subroutines `sumIntegerMethod1` and `sumIntegerMethod2` discussed at the beginning of this chapter?

Exercises

1. Assuming a is an array of n elements, compute the time complexity of the following algorithm.

Explain how you arrive at your answer.

```
duplicate ← False
FOR i ← 0 TO n - 2
    FOR j ← i + 1 TO n - 1
        IF a [i] = a[j] THEN duplicate ← True
    ENDFOR
ENDFOR
```
[3]

2. (a) Complete the following table showing values of f(n):

n	1	2	4	8	12
$f(n) = n^2$	1	4			
$f(n) = 2^n$	2	4			
$f(n) = \log_2 n$	0	1			3.585
$f(n) = n!$	1				479,001,600

[4]

(b) Place the following algorithms in order of time complexity, with the most efficient algorithm first. [2]

Algorithm A of time complexity $O(n)$

Algorithm B of time complexity $O(2^n)$

Algorithm C of time complexity $O(\log n)$

Algorithm D of time complexity $O(n^2)$

Algorithm E of time complexity $O(n!)$

(c) Explain why algorithms with time complexity $O(n!)$ are generally considered not to be helpful in solving a problem. Under what circumstances would such an algorithm be considered? [3]

(d) The merge sort algorithm has time complexity $O(n \log n)$. For a list of 1,024 items in random sequence, is this algorithm more or less efficient than a sort algorithm of time complexity $O(n^2)$? Explain your answer, with the aid of an example. [3]

Chapter 46 – Searching and sorting

Objectives

- Know and be able to trace and analyse the time complexity of the linear search and binary search algorithms
- Be able to trace and analyse the time complexity of the binary tree search algorithm
- Know and be able to explain and trace and analyse the time complexity of the bubble sort algorithm
- Be able to trace and analyse the time complexity of the merge sort algorithm

Linear search

Sometimes it is necessary to search for items in a file, or in an array in memory. If the items are not in any particular sequence, the data items have to be searched one by one until the required one is found or the end of the list is reached. This is called a **linear search**.

The following algorithm for a linear search of a list or array `alist` (indexed from 0) returns the index of `itemSought` if it is found, -1 otherwise.

```
SUB linearSearch(alist,itemSought)
   index ← -1
   i ← 0
   found ← False
   WHILE i < length(alist) AND NOT found
      IF alist[i] = itemSought THEN
         index ← i
         found ← True
      ENDIF
      i ← i + 1
   ENDWHILE
   RETURN index
ENDSUB
```

8-46

Q1: What is the maximum number of items that would have to be examined to find a particular item in a linear search of one million items? What is the average number that would have to be searched?

Time complexity of linear search

We can determine the algorithm's efficiency in terms of execution time, expressed in Big-O notation. To do this, you need to compute the number of basic operations that the algorithm will require for n items. The loop is performed n times for a list of length n, and the basic operation in the loop is the `IF` statement, giving a total of n steps in the algorithm. The time complexity of the algorithm basically depends on *how often the loop has to be performed in the worst-case scenario*.

Therefore, the time complexity of the linear search is O(n).

Binary search

The binary search is a much more efficient method of searching a list for an item than a linear search, but crucially, the items in the list must be sorted. If they are not sorted, a linear search is the only option.

Suppose the items to be searched are held in an ordered array. The ordered array is divided into three parts; a middle item, the first part of the array starting at aList[0] up to the middle item and the second part starting after the middle item and ending with the final item in the list. The middle item is examined to see if it is equal to the sought item.

If it is not, then if it is greater than the sought item, the second half of the array is of no further interest. The number of items being searched is therefore halved and the process repeated until the last item is examined, with either the first or second half of the array of items being eliminated at each pass. A subroutine for a binary search on an array of n items in an array aList is given below.

first, last and midpoint are integer variables used to index elements of the array. The variable first will start at 0, the beginning of the array. The variable last starts at len(aList) − 1, the last array index.

```
SUB binarySearch(aList, itemSought)
    found ← False
    index ← -1
    first ← 0
    last ← len(aList) - 1
    WHILE first <= last AND found = False
        midpoint ← Integer part of ((first + last) / 2)
        IF aList[midpoint] = itemSought THEN
            found ← True
            index ← midpoint
        ELSE
            IF aList[midpoint] < itemSought THEN
                first ← midpoint + 1
            ELSE
                last ← midpoint - 1
            ENDIF
        ENDIF
    ENDWHILE
    RETURN index     #index = -1 if key not found
ENDSUB
```

Time complexity of binary search

The binary search halves the search area with each execution of the loop – an excellent example of a **divide and conquer** strategy. If we start with n items, there will be approximately n/2 items left after the first comparison, n/4 after 2 comparisons, n/8 after 3 comparisons, and $n/2^i$ after i comparisons. The number of comparisons needed to end up with a list of just one item is i where $n/2^i = 1$. One further comparison would be needed to check if this item is the one being searched for or not.

Solving this equation for i, $\qquad n = 2^i$

Taking the logarithm of each side, $\qquad \log_2 n = i \log_2 2$ giving $i = \log_2 n$ (since $\log_2 2 = 1$)

Therefore, the binary search is O(log n).

Q2: An array contains 12 numbers 5, 13, 16, 19, 26, 35, 37, 57, 86, 90, 93, 98

Trace through the binary search algorithm to find how many items have to be examined before the number 90 is found. The first row of the trace table is filled in below.

itemSought	index	found	first	last	midpoint	aList(midpoint)
90	-1	false	0	11	5	35

Q3: What is the maximum number of items that would have to be examined to find a particular item in a binary search of one million items?

A recursive algorithm

The basic concept of the binary search is in fact recursive, and a recursive algorithm is given below. The procedure calls itself, eventually "unwinding" when the procedure ends. When recursion is used there must always be a condition that if true, causes the program to terminate the recursive procedure, or the recursion will continue forever.

Once again, `first`, `last` and `midpoint` are integer variables used to index elements of the array, with `first` starting at 0 and `last` starting at the upper limit of the array index.

```
SUB binarySearch (aList, itemSought, first, last)
   IF last < first THEN
      RETURN -1
   ELSE
      midpoint ← integer part of (first + last)/2
      IF aList[midpoint] > itemSought THEN #key is in first half of list
         RETURN binarySearch(aList, itemSought, first, midpoint-1)
      ELSE
         IF aList[midpoint] < itemSought THEN
            RETURN binarySearch(aList, itemSought,  midpoint+1, last)
         ELSE
            RETURN midpoint
         ENDIF
      ENDIF
   ENDIF
ENDSUB
```

8-46

Q4: What condition(s) will cause a value to be returned from the subroutine to the calling program?

Binary tree search

The recursive algorithm for searching a binary tree is similar to the binary search algorithm above, except that instead of looking at the midpoint of a list, or a subset of the list, on each pass, half of the tree or subtree is eliminated each time its root is examined. In the tree below, a maximum of 4 nodes has to be examined to find a value or return "not found". The time complexity is the same as the binary search, i.e. O(log n).

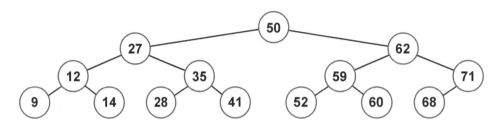

```
SUB binarySearchTree(itemSought,currentNode)
   IF currentNode = None THEN
      RETURN False
   ELSE
      IF itemSought = item at currentNode THEN
         RETURN True
      ELSE
         IF itemSought < item at currentNode THEN
            IF left child exists THEN
               RETURN binarySearchTree (itemSought, left child)
            ELSE
               RETURN False
            ENDIF
            IF right child exists THEN
               RETURN binarySearchTree (itemSought, right child)
            ELSE
               RETURN False
            ENDIF
         ENDIF
      ENDIF
   ENDIF
ENDSUB
```

Sorting algorithms

The **bubble sort** (see Chapter 9) is the simplest but by far the most inefficient sorting algorithm. It uses two nested loops to sort n items:

```
FOR i = 0 to n-2
   FOR j = 0 to n-i-2
      IF item[j] > item[j+1] THEN swap the items
   ENDFOR
ENDFOR
```

The IF statement in the inner loop is performed (n-1) + (n-2) + ... + 2 + 1 times. This is equal to ½n(n-1), or $\frac{1}{2}n^2 - \frac{1}{2}n$, using the formula for an arithmetic progression. Its time complexity is therefore a quadratic function involving n^2, i.e. $O(n^2)$, ignoring the coefficient of n and the less dominant term in n.

8-46

Merge sort

The merge sort uses a **divide and conquer** approach and is far more efficient for a large number of items. The list is successively divided in half, forming two sublists, until each sublist is of length one. The sublists are then sorted and merged into larger sublists until they are recombined into a single sorted list. The basic steps are:

- Divide the unsorted list into n sublists, each containing one element

- Repeatedly merge sublists to produce new sorted sublists until there is only one sublist remaining. This is the sorted list.

The merge process is shown graphically below for a list is in the initial sequence 5 3 2 7 9 1 3 8.

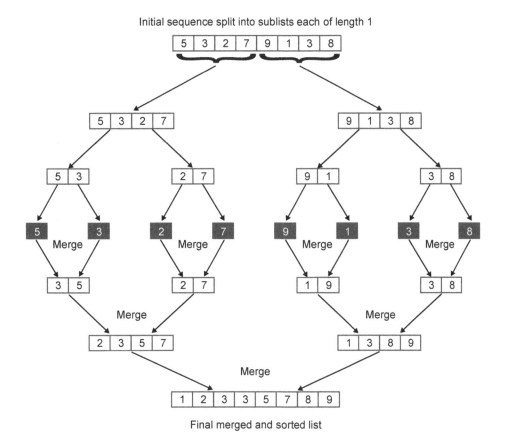

Initial sequence split into sublists each of length 1

Final merged and sorted list

8-46

The list is first split into sublists each containing one element.

The merge process merges each pair of sublists into the correct sequence. Taking for example two lists: `leftlist = [2, 3]` and `rightlist = [1, 3]`, the merge process works like this:

1. Compare the first item in `leftlist` with the first element in `rightlist`

2. If item in `leftlist` < item in `rightlist`, add item from `leftlist` to `mergedlist` and read the next item from `leftlist`

3. Otherwise, add item from `rightlist` to `mergedlist` and read the next item from `rightlist`

4. Once one list is empty, any remaining items are copied into the merged list

5. Repeat from Step 2 until all items are in `mergedlist`

The process is then repeated for each pair of sublists until the lists are merged into the final sorted list.

An algorithm for the merge sort is given below.

```
SUB mergeSort(mergelist)
   IF len(mergelist) > 1 THEN
      mid ← len(mergelist) div 2  #performs integer division
      lefthalf ← mergelist[:mid]   #left half of mergelist into lefthalf
      righthalf ← mergelist[mid:] #right half of mergelist into righthalf
      mergeSort(lefthalf)
      mergeSort(righthalf)
      i ← 0
      j ← 0
      k ← 0
      WHILE i < len(lefthalf) and j < len(righthalf)
         IF lefthalf[i] < righthalf[j] THEN
            mergelist[k] ← lefthalf[i]
            i ← i + 1
         ELSE
            mergelist[k] ← righthalf[j]
            j ← j + 1
         ENDIF
         k ← k + 1
      ENDWHILE
      #check if left half has elements not merged
      WHILE i < len(lefthalf)
         mergelist[k] ← lefthalf[i]    #if so, add to mergelist
         i ← i + 1
         k ← k + 1
      ENDWHILE
      #check if rt half has elements not merged
      WHILE j < len(righthalf)
         mergelist[k] ← righthalf[j]  #if so, add to mergelist
         j ← j + 1
         k ← k + 1
      ENDWHILE
   ENDIF
ENDSUB
#****** MAIN PROGRAM *******
mergelist ← [5, 3, 2, 7, 9, 1, 3, 8]
mergeSort(mergelist)
print(mergelist)
```

8-46

Q5: The following list of numbers is to be sorted using a merge sort.

[54, 36, 66, 78, 64, 19, 42, 44, 51, 89, 72, 62, 22, 67, 81, 79]

Which answer below shows the first two lists to be merged?

a. [44] and [51]

b. [54] and [36]

c. [54, 36] and [66, 78]

d. [19, 36, 42, 44, 54, 64, 66, 78] and [22, 51, 62, 67, 72, 79, 81, 89]

Q6: Draw a graphical representation of how a list [5, 3, 9, 4, 2, 6, 1] is first split into halves until each sublist contains one item, and then the sublists are merged to become the sorted list.

Time complexity of merge sort

The merge sort is another example of a divide and conquer algorithm, but in this case, there are n sublists to be merged, so the time complexity has to be multiplied by a factor of n.

The time complexity is therefore O(nlog n).

Space complexity

The amount of resources such as memory that an algorithm requires, known as the **space complexity**, is also a consideration when comparing the efficiency of algorithms. The bubble sort, for example, requires n memory locations for a list of size n. The merge sort, on the other hand, requires additional memory to hold the left half and right half of the list, so takes much more memory space.

8-46

Exercises

1. There are many methods of sorting a set of records into ascending order of key. What factors would you consider in deciding which of these methods is the most suitable for a particular application?   [2]

2. The binary search method can be used to search for an item in an ordered list.

(a) Show how the binary search method works by writing numbers on Figure 1 below to indicate which values would be examined to determine if the name "Richard" appears in the list.

Write the number "1" by the first value to be examined, "2" by the second value to be examined and so on.

Figure 1

Position	Value	Order examined in
1	Adam	
2	Alex	
3	Anna	
4	Hon	
5	Mohammed	
6	Moonis	
7	Niraj	
8	Philip	
9	Punit	
10	Ravi	
11	Richard	
12	Timothy	
13	Tushara	
14	Uzair	
15	Zara	

[3]

(b) A different list contains 137 names.

What is the maximum number of names that would need to be accessed to determine if the name "Rachel" appears in the list?   [1]

(c) Which of the following is the order of time complexity of the binary search method?

$O(\log_2 n)$ $O(n)$ $O(n^2)$ [1]

AQA Unit 3 Qu 1 June 2011

8-46

Chapter 47 – Graph-traversal algorithms

Objectives

- Be able to trace depth-first and breadth-first algorithms
- Describe typical applications of each

Graph traversals

There are two ways to traverse a graph so that every node is visited. Each of them uses a supporting data structure to keep track of which nodes have been visited, and which node to visit next.

- A **depth-first** traversal uses a **stack**, which is implemented automatically during execution of a recursive routine to hold local variables, parameters and return addresses each time a subroutine is called (see Chapter 39). Alternatively, a non-recursive routine could be written and the stack maintained as part of the routine.

- A **breadth-first** traversal uses a **queue.**

Depth-first traversal

In this traversal, we go as far down one route as we can before backtracking and taking the next route.

The following recursive subroutine dfs is called initially from the main program, which passes it a graph, defined here as an **adjacency list** (see Chapter 41) and implemented as a dictionary with nodes A, B, C,... as keys, and neighbours of each node as data. Thus if "A" is the current vertex, graph["A"] will return the list ["B","D","E"] with reference to the algorithm below and the graph overleaf.

The calling program also passes an empty list of visited nodes and a starting vertex.

Check the graph in Step 1 on the next page to verify that it corresponds to the nodes and their neighbours. There are different ways of drawing the graph but logically they should all be equivalent!

```
GRAPH = { "A":["B","D","E"],  "B":["A","C","D"],  "C":["B","G"],
          "D":["A","B","E","F"], "E":["A","D"] , "F":["D"], "G":["C"]}
visitedList = []      #an empty list of visited nodes

SUB dfs(graph, currentVertex, visited)
   append currentVertex to list of visited nodes
   FOR vertex in graph[currentVertex]  #check neighbours of currentVertex
      IF vertex NOT IN visited THEN
         dfs(graph, vertex, visited) #recursive call
#stack will store return address, parameters and local variables
      ENDIF
   ENDFOR
   RETURN visited
ENDSUB

#main program
traversal = dfs(GRAPH, "A", visitedList)
OUTPUT "Nodes visited in this order: ", traversal
```

8-47

It is easiest to understand how this works by looking at the graphs below. This shows the state of the **stack** (here it just shows the current node when a recursive call is made), and the contents of the **visited** list. Each visited node is coloured dark blue.

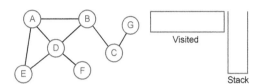

1. Start the routine with an empty stack and an empty list of visited nodes.

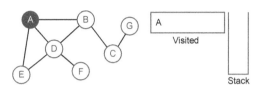

2. Visit A, add it to the visited list. Colour it to show it has been visited.

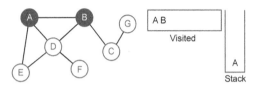

3. Push A onto the stack to keep track of where we have come from and visit A's first neighbour, B. Add it to the visited list. Colour it to show it has been visited.

4. Push B onto the stack and from B, visit the next unvisited node, C. Add it to the visited list. Colour it to show it has been visited.

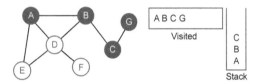

5. Push C onto the stack and from C, visit the next unvisited node, G. Add it to the visited list. Colour it to show it has been visited.

6. At G, there are no unvisited nodes so we backtrack. Pop the previous node C off the stack and return to C

7. At C, all adjacent nodes have been visited, so backtrack again. Pop B off the stack and return to B.

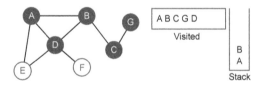

8. Push B back onto the stack to keep track of where we have come from and visit D. Add it to the visited list. Colour it to show it has been visited.

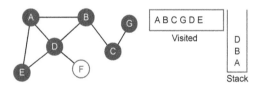

9. Push D onto the stack and visit E. Add it to the visited list. Colour it to show it has been visited.

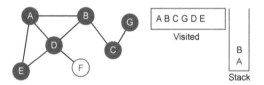

10. From E, A and D have already been visited so pop D off the stack and return to D.

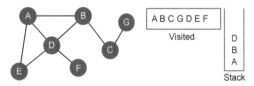

11. Push D back onto the stack and visit F. Add it to the visited list. Colour it to show it has been visited.

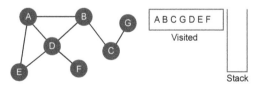

12. At F, there are no unvisited nodes so we pop D, then B, then A, whose neighbours have all been visited. The stack is now empty which means every node has been visited and the algorithm has completed.

8-47

Breadth-first traversal

With a breadth first traversal, starting at A we first visit all the nodes adjacent to A before moving to B and repeating the process for each node at this 'level', before moving to the next level. Instead of a stack, a queue is used to keep track of nodes that we still have to visit. Nodes are coloured pale blue when queued and dark blue when dequeued and added to the list of nodes that have been visited.

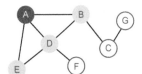

	Visited
A	Queue

1. Append A to the empty queue at the start of the routine. This will be the first visited node.

A	
	Visited
	Queue

2. Dequeue A and mark it by colouring it dark blue. Add it to the visited list.

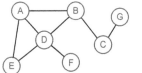

A	
	Visited
B D E	Queue

3. Queue each of A's adjacent nodes B, D and E in turn, Colour each node pale blue to show it has been queued.

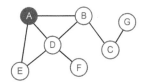

A B	
	Visited
D E	Queue

4. We've now finished with A, so dequeue the first item in the queue, which is B. Mark it by colouring it dark blue and add it to the visited list.

A B	
	Visited
D E C	Queue

5. Queue B's remaining neighbour C. Colour it pale blue to show it has been queued.

A B D	
	Visited
E C	Queue

6. B's neighbours are all coloured, so dequeue the first item in the queue, which is D. Mark it by colouring it dark blue and add it to the visited list.

A B D	
	Visited
E C F	Queue

7. D's adjacent node E has already been queued and coloured. Add D's adjacent node F to the queue. Colour it pale blue to show it has been queued.

A B D E	
	Visited
C F	Queue

8. Dequeue the first item, E. Mark it by colouring it dark blue and add it to the visited list.

A B D E C	
	Visited
F	Queue

9. E's neighbours are all coloured, so dequeue the next item, C. Mark it by colouring it dark blue and add it to the visited list.

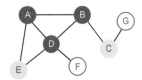

A B D E C	
	Visited
F G	Queue

10. Add C's adjacent node G to the queue and colour it pale blue to show it has been queued.

A B D E C F	
	Visited
G	Queue

11. C's neighbours are all coloured now, so dequeue F, mark it by colouring it dark blue and add it to the visited list.

A B D E C F G	
	Visited
	Queue

12. Finally, dequeue G, mark it by colouring it dark blue and add it to the visited list. The queue is now empty and all the nodes have been visited.

8-47

245

Note that we need to distinguish between a *dequeued* vertex that is added to the visited list and whose neighbours we are examining, which we colour dark blue, and *neighbours* of the current vertex, which we put in the queue and colour pale blue to show they have been queued but not visited.

Pseudocode algorithm for breadth-first traversal

The following algorithm assumes you are starting from a vertex `currentVertex`. The queue q is a dynamic data structure implemented for example as a list. A second list called `visitedNodes` holds the nodes that have been visited. Colours Black, Grey and White are more traditional in this algorithm than Dark Blue, Pale Blue and white so are used here – the diagrams are clearer in colour!

The breadth-first traversal is an iterative, rather than a recursive routine. The first node ('A' in this example), is appended to the empty queue as soon as the subroutine is entered. A Python definition of the graph as a dictionary is given below for interest, but is not directly used in the pseudocode, as implementations will vary in different languages.

```
GRAPH = {
    "A": {"colour": "White", "neighbours": ["B", "D", "E"]},
    "B": {"colour": "White", "neighbours": ["A", "D", "C"]},
    "C": {"colour": "White", "neighbours": ["B", "G"]},
    "D": {"colour": "White", "neighbours": ["A", "B", "E", "F"]},
    "E": {"colour": "White", "neighbours": ["A", "D"]},
    "F": {"colour": "White", "neighbours": ["D"]},
    "G": {"colour": "White", "neighbours": ["C"]}
}
```

8-47

```
SUB bfs(graph, vertex)
    queue   ← []      #an empty queue
    visited ← []      #an empty list of visited nodes
    enqueue vertex
    WHILE queue NOT empty
        dequeue item and put in currentNode
        set colour of currentNode to "Black"
        append currentNode to visited
        FOR each neighbour of currentNode
            IF colour of neighbour = "White" THEN
                enqueue neighbour
                set colour of neighbour to "Grey"
            ENDIF
        ENDFOR
    ENDWHILE
    RETURN visited
ENDSUB

#main
visited ← bfs(GRAPH, "A")
OUTPUT "List of nodes visited: ", visited
```

Applications of depth-first search

Applications of the depth-first search include the following:

- In scheduling jobs where a series of tasks is to be performed, and certain tasks must be completed before the next one begins.

- In solving problems such as mazes, which can be represented as a graph

Finding a way through a maze

A depth-first search can be used to find a way out of a maze. Junctions where there is a choice of route in the maze are represented as nodes on a graph.

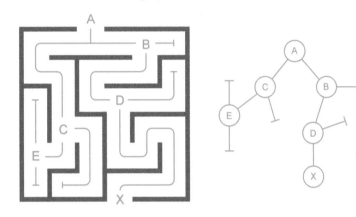

Q1: (a) Redraw the graph without showing the dead ends.

   (b) State the properties of this graph that makes it a tree.

   (c) Complete the table below to show how the graph would be represented using an adjacency matrix.

8-47

	A	B	C	D	E	X
A						
B						
C						
D						
E						
X						

Q2: Draw a graph representing the following maze. Show the dead ends on your graph.

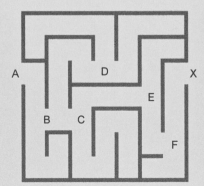

Applications of breadth-first search

Breadth-first searches are used to solve many real-life problems. For example:

- A major application of a breadth-first search is to find the *shortest* path between two points A and B, and this will be explained in detail in the next chapter. Finding the shortest path is important in, for example, GPS navigation systems and computer networks.

- Facebook. Each user profile is regarded as a node or vertex in the graph, and two nodes are connected if they are each other's friends. This example is considered in more depth in Chapter 72, Big Data.

- Web crawlers. A web crawler can analyse all the sites you can reach by following links randomly on a particular website.

Exercises

1. (a) Name the supporting data structure which is commonly used when traversing a graph

    (i)   depth-first   [1]

    (ii)   breadth-first   [1]

 (b) Show the order in which vertices in the following graph are visited, starting at A, using

    (i)   depth-first traversal   [3]

    (ii)   breadth-first traversal   [3]

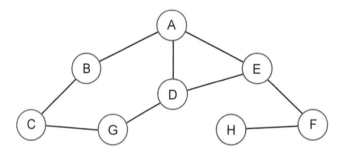

 (c) (i)   Explain why the graph above is not a tree. Which edges would need to be removed for it to be a tree?   [2]

    (ii)   Show, by traversing the tree below using a pre-order traversal and writing the nodes in the order that they are visited, that a pre-order tree traversal is equivalent to a depth-first graph traversal.   [2]

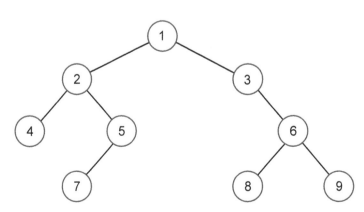

8-47

Chapter 48 – Optimisation algorithms

Objectives

- Understand and be able to trace Dijkstra's shortest path algorithm
- Be aware of applications of shortest path algorithm

Optimisation problems

We increasingly rely on computers to find the optimum solution to a range of different problems. For example:

- scheduling aeroplanes and staff so that air crews always have the correct minimum rest time between flights
- finding the best move in a chess problem
- timetabling classes in schools and colleges
- finding the shortest path between two points – for building circuit boards, route planning, communications networks and many other applications

Finding the shortest path from A to B has numerous applications in everyday life and in computer-related problems. For example, if you visit a site like Google Maps to get directions from your current location to a particular destination, you probably want to know the shortest route. The software that finds it for you will use representations of street maps or roads as **graphs**, with estimated driving times or distances as **edge weights**.

8-48

Dijkstra's shortest path algorithm

Dijkstra (pronounced dike-stra) lived from 1930 to 2002. He was a Dutch computer scientist who received the Turing award in 1972 for fundamental contributions to developing programming languages. He wrote a paper in 1968 which was published under the heading "GO TO Statement Considered Harmful" and was an advocate of **structured programming**.

Dijkstra's algorithm is designed to find the shortest path between one particular start node and every other node in a weighted graph. The algorithm is similar to a breadth first search, but uses a priority queue rather than a FIFO queue.

The weights could represent, for example, distances or time taken to travel between towns, or the cost of travel between airports.

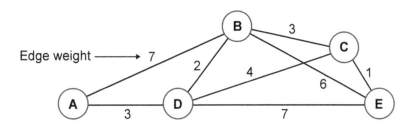

The algorithm

The algorithm works as follows:

```
Assign a temporary distance value to every node, starting with zero for
the initial node and infinity for every other node
Add all the vertices to a priority queue, sorted by current distance.
(This puts the initial node at the front, the rest in random order.)
WHILE the queue is not empty
        remove the vertex u from the front of the queue
        FOR each unvisited neighbour w of the current vertex u
            newDistance ← distanceAtU + distanceFromUtoW
            IF newDistance < distanceAtW THEN
                distanceAtW ← newDistance
                change position of w in priority queue to reflect new
                                               distance to w

            ENDIF
        ENDFOR
ENDWHILE
```

Example

In the figure below, A is the start node. A temporary distance value has been assigned to every node, starting with zero for the start node and infinity for every other node.

The priority queue is shown beside the graph, and it is kept in order of vertices with the shortest known distance from A. To start with, A is at the front, and the other nodes are in random order, in this case alphabetical.

The vertices are coloured.

- White vertices have not been visited and their distances remain at infinity.

- Pale blue vertices have been partially explored. A tentative distance to them has been found but all possible paths to them have not yet been explored, so this distance cannot be guaranteed to be the shortest one and they remain in the queue.

- Dark blue vertices have been removed from the queue and their minimum distance from A has been found. These vertices are described as having being visited.

Start at A, remove it from the front of the queue and shade it dark blue to show it has been visited

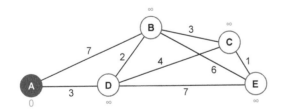

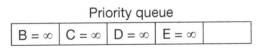

Priority queue

| B = ∞ | C = ∞ | D = ∞ | E = ∞ | |

Node A has two neighbours B and D. Shade each of these pale blue to show they have been partially explored, and calculate new distance values for nodes B and D by taking the distance value at A (i.e. zero) and adding it to the edge weight between A and B, A and D.

Since all these values are less than infinity, update the distances at B and D. Distance at D is less than distance at B, so move D to the front of the priority queue.

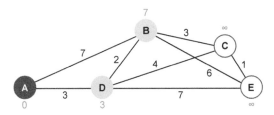

D = 3	B = 7	C = ∞	E = ∞	

Remove D from the front of the queue. Shade it dark blue to show it has been visited. Shade D's neighbours C and E pale blue to show they have been partially explored.

Now calculate new values for the unvisited neighbours of D, namely B, C and E. The distance between D and B is 2, and this is added to the edge weight between D and A. 3 + 2 = 5 so the distance value at B is changed to the new lowest value, 5.

The current tentative distance ∞ at C is replaced with 3 + 4 = 7, at E is replaced with 3 + 7 = 10.

The order of nodes in the priority queue does not need to be changed since B, the node with the smallest current distance from A, is already at the front.

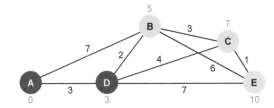

B = 5	C = 7	E = 10		

Remove B from the priority queue. Shade B dark blue to show it has been visited.

At B, the values at C and E are calculated as 5 + 3 = 8 and 5 + 6 = 11 respectively, but these are both greater than the tentative values already there, so these values are not changed.

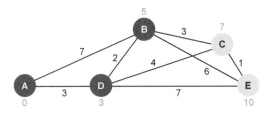

C = 7	E = 10			

Remove C from the queue and shade it dark blue to show it has been visited. The distance to E via C will be calculated as 7 + 1 = 8. This is less than current tentative distance to E (10) so will replace it.

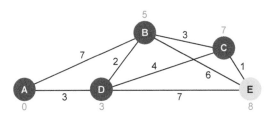

E = 8				

Remove E from the queue. It has no unvisited neighbours, so there are no new distances to calculate. Shade E dark blue.

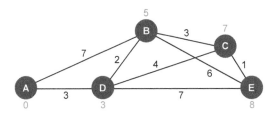

The queue is empty, all the nodes have now been visited so the algorithm ends.

We have found the shortest distance from A to every other node, and the shortest distance from A is marked in blue at each node.

Q1: Copy the graph below and use the method above to trace the shortest path from A to all other nodes. Write the shortest distance at each node.

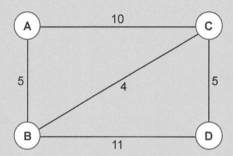

Q2: Use a similar method to trace the shortest path from A to all other nodes. Write the shortest distance at each node. What is the shortest distance from A to G?

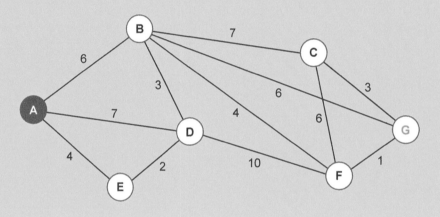

8-48

Exercises

1. (a) What is the purpose of Dijkstra's shortest path algorithm? [2]

(b) Describe briefly **two** applications of the algorithm. [4]

(c) The weighted graph (Figure 1) shows distances between each of the graph's vertices.

Copy Figure 1 and show the tentative distances from the starting node A allocated to each node after nodes B and D have been visited (dequeued and finished with) using Dijkstra's algorithm. [4]

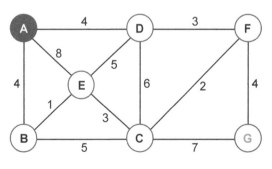

Figure 1

2. The following graph shows distances between five cities. Dijkstra's shortest path algorithm is used to find the shortest distance between Liverpool and each of the other cities. The algorithm is given below.

```
Assign a temporary distance value to every node, starting with zero
for the initial node and infinity for every other node

Add all the vertices to a priority queue, sorted by current
distance. (This puts the initial node at the front, the rest, which
all start with temporary distances of infinity, in random order.)

WHILE the queue is not empty
    remove the vertex u from the front of the queue
    FOR each unvisited neighbour w of the current vertex u
        newDistance ← distanceAtU + distanceFromUtoW
        IF newDistance < distanceAtW THEN
            distanceAtW ← newDistance
            change position of w in priority queue to reflect new
                                            distance to w
        ENDIF
    ENDFOR
ENDWHILE
```

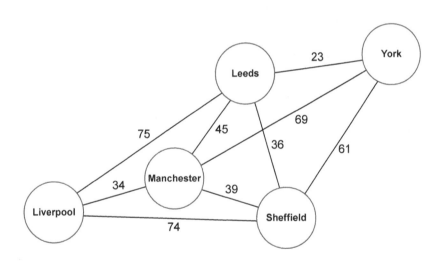

The following table represents the distances after the first statement in the algorithm is executed.

Liverpool	Leeds	Manchester	Sheffield	York
0	∞	∞	∞	∞

(a)   Complete the following table after **one** iteration of the WHILE loop in the above algorithm.   [3]

Liverpool	Leeds	Manchester	Sheffield	York

(b)   Complete the table after the **second** iteration of the WHILE loop.   [2]

Liverpool	Leeds	Manchester	Sheffield	York

Chapter 49 – Limits of computation

Objectives

- Be aware that algorithmic complexity and hardware impose limits on what can be computed

- Know that algorithms may be classified as being either tractable or intractable

- Be aware that some problems cannot be solved algorithmically

- Describe the Halting problem, and understand its significance for computation

Does every computational problem have a solution?

In this chapter we will look at the limits of computation. Some problems may be theoretically soluble by computer but if they take millions of years to solve, they are in a practical sense, insoluble. Cracking a password of 10 or more characters consisting of a random mix of upper and lowercase letters, numbers and symbols is one example.

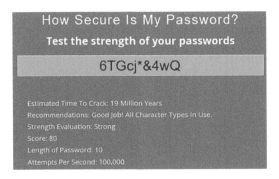

How secure is my password? www.roboform.com

The travelling salesman problem

This is a very well-known optimisation problem. It poses the question "Given a list of towns and the distances between each pair of towns, what is the shortest possible route that the salesman can use to visit each town exactly once and return to the starting point?" This is different from finding the shortest path from A to B. This problem has many applications in fields such as planning, logistics, the manufacture of microchips and DNA sequencing.

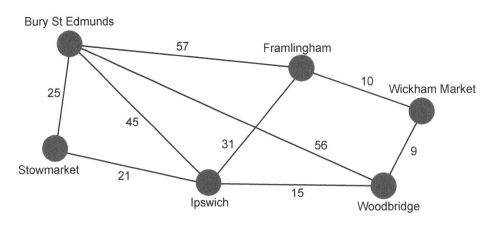

To solve the problem, we could look first at a **brute-force** method, testing out every combination of routes.

With just five cities, the number of possible routes is: $4! = 4 \times 3 \times 2 \times 1 = 24$.

A computer could calculate the best route in a fraction of a second.

Q1: How many different routes are there for (a) 10 cities? (b) 20 cities? (c) 50 cities?

The problem is **computationally difficult** because it will take a long time for a fast computer to find the optimal solution for even a relatively small number of cities, and using the brute force algorithm, the problem rapidly becomes impossible to solve within a reasonable time as the number of cities increases.

Another approach is needed, and later in this chapter we will discuss **heuristic** solutions to problems such as this one.

Tractable and intractable problems

Computer scientists are interested in the efficiency of algorithms, and whether or not it is possible, for example, to find an algorithm that will solve a problem in a "reasonable amount of time" using only a "reasonable amount of memory". Some problems in fact cannot be solved at all, however much time and memory is available. This chapter looks at how we can categorise algorithms.

A problem that has a **polynomial-time solution** or better is called a **tractable problem**. A polynomial-time solution is one of time complexity $O(n^k)$. So for example, problems which have solutions with time complexities of $O(n)$, $O(n \log n)$ and $O(n^{10})$ are all tractable.

An **intractable problem** is one that does not have a polynomial-time solution. Problems of time complexity $O(2^n)$ and $O(n!)$ are examples of intractable problems. In other words, although these problems have a theoretical solution, it is very hard to solve such a problem for a value of n of any size greater than something very small. Note that "intractable" does not mean "insoluble".

Q2: Show that for a very small value of n, a problem defined as intractable can be solved in a relatively short time.

An example of a tractable problem is: "Find the shortest path between two vertices in a given weighted graph." We saw in the last chapter that this is relatively easy to solve efficiently.

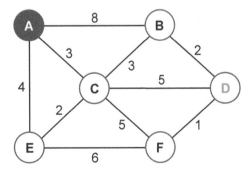

However, if we wanted to find the *longest* path between two vertices, this is a problem which can only be solved by exhaustive search – in other words, trying every option.

Comparing time complexities

The table below shows what a huge difference there is in algorithms with different orders of time complexity for different values of n.

	10	**50**	**100**	**1000**
n	10	50	100	1000
$\log_2 n$	3.3	5.64	6.65	9.97
n^2	100	2500	10,000	1 million
n^3	1000	125000	1 million	1 billion
2^n	1024	A 16-digit number	A 31-digit number	A 302-digit number
n!	3.6 million	A 65-digit number	A 161-digit number	A very, very large number!

> **Q3:** Algorithms for problems A, B and C have time complexities $O(n^3)$, $O(2^n)$, $O(n!)$. Using the table above, which of A, B, C are tractable and which are intractable?

Intractable problems, which have no efficient algorithms to solve them, are in fact quite common; so how can solutions to these problems be found?

Heuristic methods

Not all intractable problems are equally hard, and not all instances of a given intractable problem are equally hard. Brute-force algorithms are not the only option. It may be quite simple to get an approximate answer, or an answer that is good enough for a particular purpose. One approach is to find a solution which has a high probability of being correct.

Another approach is to solve a simpler or restricted version of the problem, if that is possible. This may give useful insights into possible solutions.

An approach to problem solving which employs an algorithm or methodology not guaranteed to be optimal or perfect, but is sufficient for the purpose, is called a **heuristic** approach. An adequate solution may be achieved by trading optimality, completeness, accuracy or precision for speed.

Returning to the **Travelling Salesman Problem** (TSP), a large number of heuristic solutions have been developed, the best of which (developed in 2006) can compute a solution within two or three percent of an optimal tour for as many as 85,000 "cities" or nodes.

In fields other than computer science, individuals and organisations frequently use heuristic methods in reaching decisions, and researchers have found that ignoring part of the information at hand can actually lead to more accurate decisions. Examples of a heuristic approach include using a rule of thumb, making an educated guess or an intuitive judgement, or simply using common sense.

Many **virus scanners** use heuristic rules for detecting viruses and other forms of malware. The heuristic algorithm looks for code and behaviour patterns indicative of a class or family of viruses.

Computable and non-computable problems

There are some problems which cannot be solved algorithmically. In fact, the number of things which can be computed is tiny compared with the number of things we would like to be able to compute! In the 1920s, a mathematician named David Hilbert proposed that any problem, defined properly, could be solved by writing an appropriate algorithm – i.e. that every problem was computable. In 1936 Turing was able to prove him wrong. Some problems are simply non-computable.

The fact that some problems have no solution is of significance to computer scientists. One definition of Computer Science is "the study of problems that are and that are not computable", or the study of the existence and the nonexistence of algorithms.

A non-computable problem sometimes appears in the form of a paradox. For example:

Suppose in a certain town there is just one barber, who is male. Every man in the town is clean-shaven, and he keeps himself this way by doing either of the following (but not both):

1. shaving himself, or

2. going to the barber

Another way of putting this is to say that the barber is a man in town who shaves only those men in the town who do not shave themselves.

Who shaves the barber?

Q4: Can you think of some categories of non-computable problem?

The Halting problem

The Halting problem is the problem of determining whether for a given input, a program will finish running or continue for ever. The problem can be represented graphically:

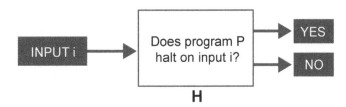

Alan Turing proved in 1936 that a machine **H** to solve the Halting problem for all possible programs and their inputs, cannot exist. It is not possible to devise a program H which can show that, given any program and its inputs, it will halt or continue for ever. It is, however, often possible to show that given a specific algorithm, it will halt for any input.

What the Halting problem shows is that there are some problems that cannot be solved by computer.

8-49

Exercises

1. The figure below illustrates the time complexity of three different algorithms, A, B and C.

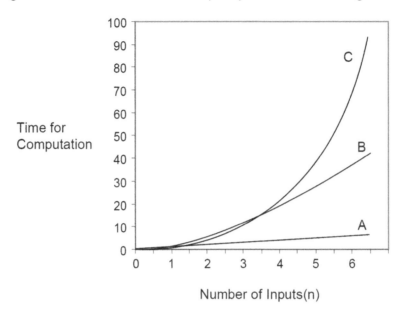

(a) The three algorithms have orders of time complexity $O(n^2)$, $O(n)$ and $O(a^n)$.

    (i)   What is the order of time complexity of algorithm C?   [1]

    (ii)   Which of the algorithms, A, B or C, is the most time efficient?   [1]

(b) The Travelling Salesman problem is intractable.

    (i)   What is meant by an intractable problem?   [2]

    (ii)   What approach might a programmer take if asked to 'solve' an intractable problem?   [2]

AQA Unit 3 Qu 5 June 2010

2. (a) Complete the missing parts of the question posed by the Halting problem in the Figure below.

    Is it possible in general to ....

    that can tell, given any program and its inputs and without

    .... whether the

    given program with the given inputs will halt?

    [2]

(b) What is the significance of the Halting problem?   [1]

AQA Unit 3 Qu 11 June 2012

8-49

Section 9

Regular languages

In this section:

9

Chapter 50 – Mealy machines

Objectives

- Be able to draw and interpret simple state transition diagrams for FSMs with no output and with output
- Be able to draw and interpret simple state transition tables for FSMs with no output and with output

Finite state machines

A finite state machine (FSM) which does not have output is sometimes referred to as a **finite state automaton.** (These were covered in Chapter 12 and you should refer back to this chapter for more detail.) An FSM is an abstract representation or model of computation used in designing computer systems and logic circuits, and one which can also be used to check the syntax of programming languages.

This chapter gives a brief revision of the concepts previously covered in Chapter 12 before moving on to a specific type of FSMs *with output*, known as **Mealy machines**.

State transition diagrams

State transition diagrams use circles to represent the states that a system may be in, and arrows to represent the transitions between states. One of the states is a **start state**, shown with an arrow pointing to it, and one or more of the states is an **accept state**, shown as a double circle.

The finite state automaton produces a Yes or No answer to the question: does the input sequence move from the start state to an accept state by any of the possible paths?

Example 1

The finite state diagram below accepts certain combinations of the letters a and b, and rejects others. Which of the following combinations of letters are accepted?

baabb   aaabb   aaaa   abba   abb   baa

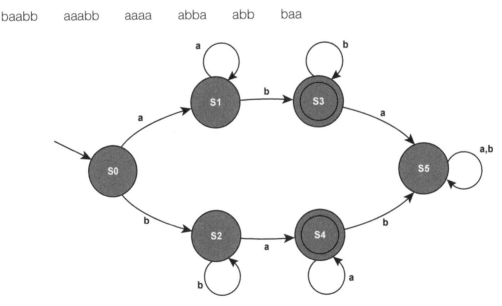

Answer: aaabb, abb, baa. These are the only three combinations that end at an accept state, S3 or S4.

State transition tables

A state transition table is an alternative way of representing an FSM, showing in tabular form the current state and the next state for each input. Here is the state transition table for the example above.

Current state	Next state	
	Input = a	Input = b
S0	S1	S2
S1	S1	S3
S2	S4	S2
S3	S5	S3
S4	S4	S5
S5	S5	S5

Mealy machines

A **Mealy machine** is a type of FSM with an output, named after its inventor George Mealy. A Mealy machine has outputs that are determined **both by its current state and the current input**. For each state and input, no more than one transition is possible.

Example 2

The controller for a vending machine is implemented as a Mealy machine as shown in the finite state diagram below. The initial state is shown with an arrow, and each transition shows both the input and the output. A packet of crisps will be dispensed when the customer has inserted three 10p coins or a 10p coin and a 20p coin. If two 20p coins are inserted, the machine will give 10p change. For example, 10p/00 means that 10p has been input and the controller does not dispense the packet of crisps and does not give change. 20p/11 means that 20p has been inserted and the machine dispenses the crisps and gives change. A Reset button gives change if the customer presses it when they have entered less than 30p.

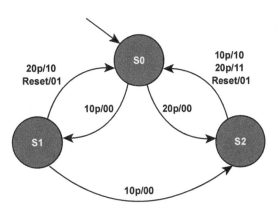

The transition table representing this Mealy machine is as follows:

Input	Current state	Output	Next state
10p	S0	00	S1
20p	S0	00	S2
10p	S1	00	S2
20p	S1	10	S0
10p	S2	10	S0
20p	S2	11	S0
Reset	S1	01	S0
Reset	S2	01	S0

Q1: What does an output of 10 mean?

Example 3

The FSM below represents a Mealy machine which accepts any number of inputs of 0 or 1. If the last two symbols input are 00 or 11, the final output is **y** (yes), otherwise the final output is **n** (no).

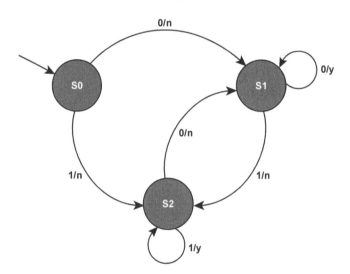

The corresponding state transition table is shown below.

Input	Current state	Output	Next state
0	S0	n	S1
1	S0	n	S2
0	S1	y	S1
1	S1	n	S2
0	S2	n	S1
1	S2	y	S2

You can show the output for any input string. Suppose you input the string 0 0 1 0 1 1.

Write these inputs down and underneath them, complete the state sequence and the output rows, column by column. Working along the row, for each input, write down the next state arrived at and the output.

Input =		0	0	1	0	1	1
State sequence =	S0	S1	S1	S2	S1	S2	S2
Output =		n	y	n	n	n	y

The final output from this string is y, at the final state S2.

Q2: Write out the state sequence for the input 1 0 1 1 0 1. What is the final state and what is the final output?

Applications of Mealy machines

Mealy machines can provide a simple model for cipher machines. Given a string of letters (a sequence of inputs), a Mealy machine can be designed to give a ciphered string (a sequence of outputs). They can also be used to represent traffic lights, timers, vending machines, and basic electronic circuits.

Example 4

This example shows a Mealy machine that represents an exclusive OR of the two most recent values input.

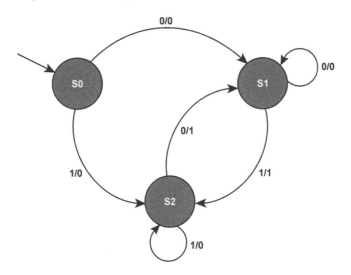

Q3: Complete the state transition table for the FSM given above.

Input	Current state	Output	Next state
0	S0	0	S1
1			
0			
1			
0			
1			

Q4: Write out the state sequence for the input string 001001.

Exercises

1. A Mealy machine is to be designed so that its final output is a 1 when at least three ones have been entered in sequence.

(a) With the aid of the state transition table below, draw the finite state diagram representing the Mealy machine. [3]

Input	Current state	Output	Next state
0	S0	0	S0
1	S0	0	S1
0	S1	0	S0
1	S1	0	S2
0	S2	0	S0
1	S2	1	S2

(b) Write the state sequence showing the output for each of the following input sequences:

   (i)   110111 [2]

   (ii) 101101 [2]

2. The following Mealy machine accepts as input a string of binary digits. The output is the remainder, given in decimal, when the string of binary digits is divided by 5. Thus for example an input string of binary digits 10 will give an output of 2, and an input string of 1011 will output 1.

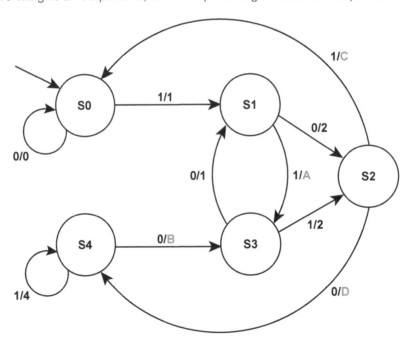

(a) What are the outputs **A**, **B**, **C** and **D**? [4]

(b) (i)   The binary string 1010011 is input. List the state sequence. [2]

   (ii) What is the output from the string? [1]

Chapter 51 – Sets

Objectives

- Be familiar with the concept of a set and the notations used for specifying a set and set comprehension
- Be familiar with the compact representation of a set
- Be familiar with the concept of finite and infinite sets, countably infinite sets, cardinality of a finite set, Cartesian product of sets
- Be familiar with the meaning of the terms subset, proper subset, countable set
- Be familiar with set operations: membership, union, intersection, difference

Definition of a set

A **set** is an unordered collection of values or symbols in which each value or symbol occurs at most once.

A set may be defined in one of three ways, and the notation used for each of these is explained below.

Defining a set by listing each member

The list of members is enclosed in curly brackets:

e.g. A = {2, 4, 6, 8}

> **Q1:** Define a set A consisting of all prime numbers between 1 and 20.

9-51

Common sets

There are some sets that are used so often that they have special names and notational conventions to identify them. These include:

- The empty set {} or $\emptyset$, which has no elements.
- The (infinite) set of natural numbers, including zero, referred to as $\mathbb{N}$ in mathematics.

  N or $\mathbb{N}$ = {0, 1, 2, 3, ...}

A **natural** number is a whole number that is used in counting. For example, five gold rings, four calling birds, three French hens. (This is sometimes defined as {1, 2, 3, ...} without including zero.)

Note that the ellipsis ("...") indicates that the set continues in the obvious way, and can be used to indicate an infinite set.

- The set of all **integers** whether positive, negative or zero:

  Z or $\mathbb{Z}$ = {..., -2, -1, 0, 1, 2, ...}

- The set of all **rational numbers Q** or $\mathbb{Q}$, i.e. any value that can be expressed as a ratio, or fraction. This includes all integer values since each can simply be expressed as 7/1 or 1076/1, to use the examples above.
- The set **R** or $\mathbb{R}$ of **real numbers** is defined as 'the set of all possible real world quantities'. This includes, for example, -10, -6.456, 0 4, 6.0, $\sqrt{2}$ and π. It does not include 'imaginary' numbers such as $\sqrt{-1}$, or infinity (∞).

> **Q2:** Define a set B of all positive integers divisible by 2.

Finite and infinite sets

A **finite set** is one whose elements can be counted off by natural numbers up to a particular number. For example, 10 is the fourth and final element of the set A = {1, 4, 6, 10}.

Another example of a finite set is the set of all odd numbers from 1 to 99, which may be specified as:

A = {1, 3, 5, …, 99}

Again, the ellipsis (…) indicates that the list continues in the obvious way.

The **cardinality** of a finite set is the number of elements in the set.

An **infinite set** may be countable or uncountable. For example, $\mathbb{N}$ (the set of natural numbers) and $\mathbb{R}$ (the set of real numbers) are examples of infinite sets, because they cannot be counted off against the set of natural numbers up to a certain number.

$\mathbb{N}$ is a **countably infinite set** because you can count the elements off against the set of natural numbers; 0, 1, 2, 3 and so on. This is in contrast to the set $\mathbb{R}$ which is not countable; you cannot list all the numbers in the set or say which is the next number.

A **countable** set is a set which can be counted off against a subset of the natural numbers, i.e. all of the natural numbers up to a fixed limit. A countably infinite set is one which can be counted off against the natural numbers but without ever stopping.

Defining a set by set comprehension

A set may be defined by **set comprehension**, using the notation shown in the example below:

$$B = \{n^2 \mid n \in \mathbb{N} \wedge n < 5\}$$

- The vertical bar | means "such that"
- The $\in$ symbol indicates membership, so $x \in \mathbb{N}$ is read as "x belongs to $\mathbb{N}$"
- $\wedge$ means "and"

Another way of writing the set B, therefore, is

$$B = \{0, 1, 4, 9, 16\}$$

9-51

> **Q3:** Given that A = $\{x \mid x \in \mathbb{N} \wedge x \geq 1\}$, complete the sentence
>   "A is the set consisting of those elements x such that …"
>
> **Q4:** Define set A = {0, 1, 8, 27, 64} using set comprehension.
>
> **Q5:** List the numbers in the following set: A = $\{\{2x \mid x \in \mathbb{N} \wedge x \geq 1 \wedge x \leq 4\}\}$

Defining a set using the compact representation

A set may be defined using the **compact representation**, as in the following example:

$$A = \{0^n 1^n \mid n\}$$

In this notation, A is the set containing all strings with an equal number of 0s and 1s.

Another way of writing this set is A = {01, 0011, 000111, 00001111, …}

> **Q6:** Using set comprehension or compact representation, define:
>   (a)   the set A consisting of all the positive integers divisible by 5.
>   (b)   the set B consisting of all positive integers between 1 and 9.
>   (c)   the set C consisting of all positive integer powers of 2.

Cartesian product of two sets

The Cartesian product of two sets A and B, written A x B and spoken "A cross B", is the set of all ordered pairs (a, b) where a is a member of A and b is a member of B.

Example: The set A is defined as A = {1, 3, 5} and the set B as B = {12, 25, 40}. The definition of set C, which is defined as A x B is written:

C = {(1, 12), (1, 25), (1, 40), (3, 12), (3, 25), (3, 40), (5, 12), (5, 25), (5, 40)}

Q7: What is the Cartesian product C of sets S1 and S2, where S1 = {4, 8, 3} and S2 = {8}?

Subsets

If every member of set A is also a member of set B, then A is a **subset** of B, written

A ⊆ B

An equivalent statement is "B is a superset of A" or "B contains A", written

B ⊇ A

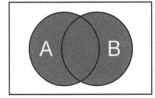

If A is a subset of, but not equal to B, then A is called a **proper subset** of B.

A ⊂ B   e.g. {0, 1, 2} ⊂ ℕ

Q8: If A is the set of prime numbers less than 10, B is the set of odd numbers less than 10 and C is the set of even numbers less than 10, which of the following statements are true?

A ⊆ B   B ⊆ A   A ⊆ C   C ⊆ A   B ⊆ C   C ⊆ B

Set membership

If A is a set and x is one of the elements of A, then x is a member of A, denoted by x ∈ A.

Set operations

There are several operations which can be used to construct new sets from given sets.

Union

Two sets A and B can be "added together", resulting in the set that contains everything in either A or B. The **union** of A and B is denoted by

A ∪ B

Examples: A = {1, 3, 5} B = {3, 4, 8}

A ∪ B = {1, 3, 4, 5, 8}

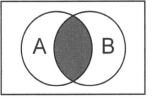

Q9: If A = {1, 3, 5}, what is in set A ∪ A?

Intersection

The **intersection** of two sets contains all the members that both sets have in common. Thus the intersection of the two sets

A = {1, 2, 3, 4, 5} and B = {1, 3, 5, 7, 9} is the set {1, 3, 5}

This is written as A ∩ B = {1, 3, 5}

Q10: If A is defined as {1, 2, 3} and B = ∅ (the empty set), define the set A ∩ B.

Difference

The **difference** of two sets is denoted by A \ B.

If A = {1, 2, 3, 4} and B = {1, 3}, then A \ B = {2, 4}

If A = {1, 2, 3, 4} and B = {1, 3, 5}, then A \ B = {2, 4}. "Subtracting" a member that is not in set A has no effect.

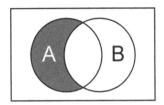

Q11: If A is the set of prime numbers less than 10 and B is the set of odd numbers less than 12, what numbers are in set C = B \ A?

Exercises

1. Give an equivalent definition of the set A = {x | x = x^2} which shows the values in the set.　　　　[1]

2. (a) What is the meaning of

   (i) A ⊆ B

   (ii) A ⊇ B?

   Give an example of each.　　　　[4]

   (b) Given that A = {2x | x ∈ ℕ} and B = {4x | x ∈ ℕ}, which of the following is true?

   (i) A ⊆ B

   (ii) A ⊇ B

   Explain how you reached this conclusion.　　　　[3]

3. The following is a list of sets.

   S1 = {1, 2, 3, 4}

   S2 = {3, 1}

   S3 = {3, 4, 5}

   S4 = {1, 2, 3, 4}

   S5 = {1}

   S6 = {2, 4}

   (a) (i) State the name of **three** proper subsets of S1.　　　　[3]

   (ii) State the name of a subset of S1 which is not a proper subset of S1.　　　　[1]

   (b) What is the Cartesian product of sets S1 and S2?　　　　[1]

   (c) Show how the set S6 can be created using the difference set operator together with two of the other sets listed.　　　　[1]

   (d) Define the following sets:

   (i) S7, which is the union of sets S1 and S3.　　　　[1]

   (ii) S8, which is the intersection of sets S1 and S3.　　　　[1]

Chapter 52 – Regular expressions

Objectives

- Understand that a regular expression is a way of describing a set
- Understand that regular expressions allow particular types of languages to be described in convenient shorthand notation
- Be able to form and use simple regular expressions for string manipulation and matching
- Be able to describe the relationship between regular expressions and finite state machines
- Be able to write a regular expression to recognise the same language as a given FSM and vice versa

What is a regular expression?

Regular expressions are a tool that enables programmers and computers to work with text patterns. They are used, for example,

- to match patterns in text files (for example when searching for a particular word in a word processing program)
- by compilers to recognise the correct form of a variable name or the syntax of a statement
- by programmers to validate user input (for example to check that a postcode or an email address is in the correct format)

Many programming languages including Python and Java support regular expressions.

A regular expression, often called a **pattern**, is an expression used to specify a set of strings that satisfy given conditions.

9-52

The most common symbols used in regular expressions are described below.

- | A vertical bar separates alternatives
- ? A question mark indicates that there are zero or one of the preceding element
- * An asterisk indicates that there are zero or more of the preceding element
- + A superscript plus sign indicates that there is one or more of the preceding element

Regular expression	Meaning	Matching strings
(Edward)|(Eddie)|(Ed)	Boolean OR; a vertical bar separates alternatives	Edward, Eddie, Ed
(D|d)is(c|k)	Parentheses are used to define the scope and precedence of the operators	"Disc", "disc", "Disk" and "disk"
Dialog(ue)?	? indicates zero or one of the preceding element	Dialog, Dialogue
ab*	* indicates there are zero or more of the preceding element	a, ab, abb,abbb, ...
a^+b	+ indicates there are one or more of the preceding element	ab, aab,aaab ...

Regular language

A language is called **regular** if it can be represented by a regular expression. A regular language can also be defined as any language that a **finite state machine** will accept. Any finite language (one containing only a finite number of words) is a regular language, since a regular expression can be created that is the union of every word in the language.

Example 1

A regular language consists of all words beginning and ending in *a*, with zero or more instances of *b* in between, e.g. aa, aba, abba, abbba.

Write a regular expression that describes this language, and draw the corresponding finite state machine (FSM).

Answer: R = ab*a. Note that the FSM is drawn with an outgoing transition from every state for every possible input symbol.

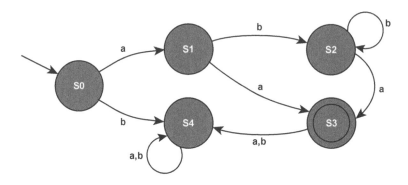

9-52

Example 2

Describe the set of strings found by 0^+1^+0 and draw the FSM.

Answer: It would find all strings with one or more zeros followed by one or more ones followed by one zero. e.g. 010, 0010, 00010, 0010, 00110

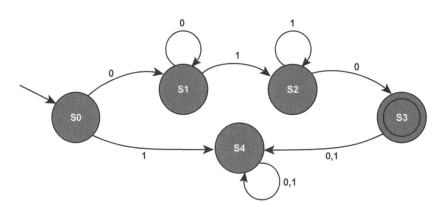

Q1: Write a regular expression to find all the occurrences of "color" or "colour" in a document.

Q2: Write a regular expression that matches any non-empty string that starts with zero or more "a"s, followed by one or more "b"s.

Q3: Which of the following strings is matched by the regular expression $Sc(o^+)(b|d)^*y$?

   Scooby   Scoby   Scddy   Scobby   Scoobdbdbdy

Draw an FSM that recognises the same language.

Finding a regular expression to express an automaton

The set of strings accepted by a language can be expressed either in graphical form as a finite state diagram, or as a regular expression. Given the regular expression, it is usually not too difficult to draw the FSM, as we have seen. The examples below give practice in writing the regular expression corresponding to a given FSM.

Example 1

Consider the FSM shown below, which has four states.

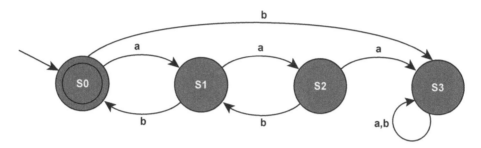

This allows an empty string and strings of the form ab, aabb and all combinations of these such as abab, aabb, aababb.

The corresponding regular expression is (a(ab)*b)*.

Q4: Write the regular expression which represents the finite state machine shown below.

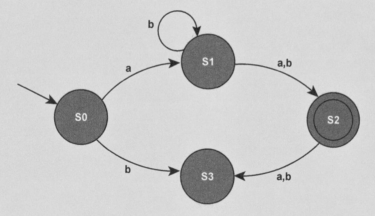

Q5: Write the regular expression which represents the finite state machine shown below.

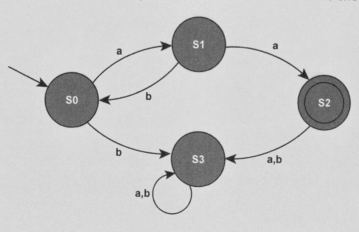

9-52

271

Exercises

1. Regular expressions can be used to search for strings. For example, de(f|g)*h⁺ matches any string that starts with *de* and is followed by zero or more instances of either *f* or *g* followed by one or more instances of *h*.

   Write regular expressions that will match:

   (a) any string that starts with a letter a, ends with a letter c and has one or more occurrences of the letter b in the middle of it, ie the expression should match the strings abc, abbc, abbbc and so on. [1]

   (b) any string that starts with either a 0 or a 1, followed by zero or more occurrences of the digit 1, ie the expression should match the strings 0, 1, 01, 11, 011 and so on. [1]

   AQA Unit 3 Qu 12 June 2012

2. Regular expressions can be used to search for strings.

   (a) For each of the following regular expressions, describe the set of strings that they would find.

   (i)   a⁺b [1]

   (ii) a?b [1]

   (iii) (ab)* [1]

   (b) Write regular expressions that match:

   (i) either Clare or Claire. [1]

   (ii) any non-empty string that:

   - starts with 10

   - has zero or more occurrences of any combination of 0 or 1 in the middle

   - ends with 01

   Example strings that the expression should match are 1001, 100010101, 101111010101001. [2]

   AQA Unit 3 Qu 9 June 2011

3. (a) Which of the following strings will be accepted by the finite state automaton shown below?

   11001   01000   101111   000110 [3]

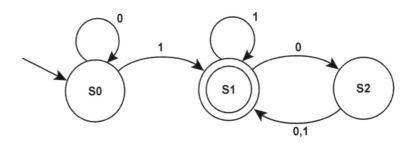

   (b) Write a regular expression to describe the language that the FSA will accept. [3]

4. Draw a four-state FSM that represents the regular expression b*ab*a. [3]

Chapter 53 – The Turing machine

Objectives

- Know that a Turing machine can be viewed as a computer with a single fixed program, expressed using
    - a finite set of states in a state transition diagram
    - a finite alphabet of symbols
    - an infinite tape with marked off squares
    - a sensing read-write head that can travel along the tape, one square at a time
- Understand the equivalence between a transition function and a state transition diagram
- Be able to:
    - represent transition rules using a transition function
    - represent transition rules using a state transition diagram
    - hand-trace simple Turing machines
- Explain the importance of Turing machines and the Universal Turing machine to the subject of computation

Alan Turing

Alan Turing (1912–1954) was a British computer scientist and mathematician, best known for his work at Bletchley Park during the Second World War. While working there, he devised an early computer for breaking German ciphers, work which probably shortened the war by two or more years and saved countless lives.

Turing was interested in the question of **computability**, and the answer to the question "Is every mathematical task computable?" In 1936 he invented a theoretical machine, which became known as the **Turing machine**, to answer this question.

The Turing machine

The Turing machine consists of an infinitely long strip of tape divided into squares. It has a read/write head that can read symbols from the tape and make decisions about what to do based on the contents of the cell and its current state.

Essentially, this is a finite state machine with the addition of an infinite memory on tape. The FSM specifies the task to be performed; it can erase or write a different symbol in the current cell, and it can move the read/write head either left or right.

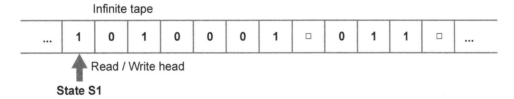

The Turing machine is an early precursor of the modern computer, with input, output and a program which describes its behaviour. Any alphabet may be defined for the Turing machine; for example a binary alphabet of 0, 1 and □ (representing a blank), as shown in the diagram above.

A Turing machine must have at least one state, known as a **halting state** or **stop state** that causes it to halt for some inputs.

Example 1

A Turing machine is designed to find the first blank cell on the tape to the right of the current position of the read/write head.

It has three states S0, S1 and S2, where S0 is the start state and S2 is the stop state. The machine's alphabet is 0, 1 and □ where □ represents a blank.

The finite state transition diagram representing the machine is shown below.

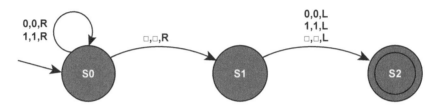

The notation (*input*, *output*, *movement*) is used in this diagram so that for example, (0, 0, R), means "If the input is 0, write a 0 and move right". (0, 1, L) means "If the input is 0, write a 1 and move left."

The string 110□□□ is on the tape, and the read-write head is positioned at the leftmost 1.

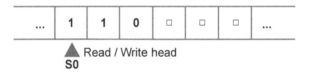

The computation of the Turing machine can be traced as follows:

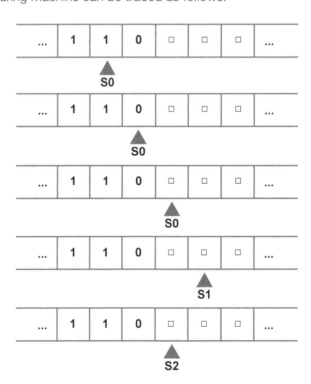

Example 2

The following state transition table shows a procedure for incrementing a binary number by 1.

Current state	Read symbol	Write symbol	Move	Next state
S0	□	□	left	S1
S0	0	0	right	S0
S0	1	1	right	S0
S1	□	1	right	S2
S1	0	1	left	S2
S1	1	0	left	S1
S2	□	□	left	S3
S2	0	0	right	S2
S2	1	1	right	S2

The machine starts in state S0 with the head at the leftmost digit on the tape holding the string 10. Trace the computation of the Turing machine.

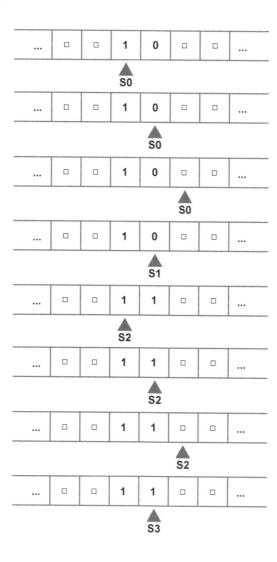

The finite state machine corresponding to the state transition diagram is given below.

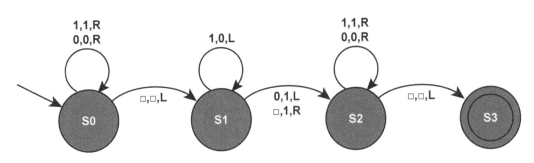

> **Q1:** Trace the computation of the Turing machine if the tape starts with the data 11 as shown below.
>
> | ... | □ | □ | 1 | 1 | □ | □ | ... |
>
> ▲
> S0
>
> (You will need to draw ten representations of the tape to complete the computation.)

Transition functions

The transition rules for any Turing machine can be expressed as a **transition function** δ. The rules are written in the form

   δ (Current State, Input symbol) = (Next State, Output symbol, Movement).

Thus the rule

   δ (S1, 0) = (S2, 1, L)

means "IF the machine is currently in state S1 and the input symbol read from the tape is 0, THEN write a 1 to the tape, and move left and change state to S2".

> **Q2:** Looking at the state transition diagram above, write the transition rules for inputs of 0, 1 and □ when the machine is in state S0.

The universal Turing machine

A Turing machine can theoretically represent any computation.

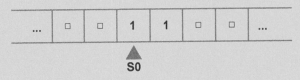

Each machine has a different program to compute the desired operation. However, the obvious problem with this is that a different machine has to be created for each operation, which is clearly impractical.

Turing therefore came up with the idea of the **Universal Turing machine**, which could be used to compute any computable sequence. He wrote: "If this machine **U** is supplied with the tape on the beginning of which is written the string of quintuples separated by semicolons of some computing machine **M**, then **U** will compute the same sequence as **M**."

U is essentially an interpreter that reads the description <M> of any arbitrary Turing machine **M** and faithfully executes operations on data precisely as **M** does. The description <M> is written at the beginning of the tape, followed by the data **D**.

Anything that a Turing machine can compute, a real computer can also compute, and so it provides a definition of what is computable. The universal machine reads both the description of the machine to be simulated, and the input to the machine, from its own tape. This model of computation is considered by some computer scientists to have been the fundamental theoretical breakthrough that led to the idea of the **stored program computer**, in which both the program and its data are held in memory.

Exercises

1. A particular Turing machine has states S1, S2, S3, and S4. S1 is the start state and S4 is the stop state. The machine uses one tape which is infinitely long in one direction to store data. The machine's alphabet is 1, □. The symbol □ is used to indicate a blank cell on the tape.

    The transition rules for this Turing machine can be expressed as a transition function δ. Rules are written in the form

    δ (Current State, Input symbol) = (Next State, Output symbol, Movement).

    So, for example, the rule

    δ (S1, 1) = (S1, 1, →)

    means

    IF   the machine is currently in state S1 and the input symbol read from the tape is 1

    THEN   the machine should remain in state S1, write a 1 to the tape and move the read/write head one cell to the right.

    The machine's transition function is defined by:

    δ (S1, 1) = (S1, 1, →)
    δ (S1, □) = (S2, □, ←)
    δ (S2, 1) = (S3, □, ←)
    δ (S3, 1) = (S4, □, ←)

    (a)   The Turing machine is carrying out a computation. The machine starts in state S1 with the string 1111 on the tape. All other cells contain the blank symbol □. The read/write head is positioned at the leftmost 1, as indicated by the arrow.

    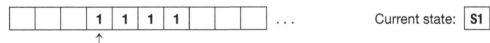

    Trace the computation of the Turing machine, using the transition function δ. Show the contents of the tape, the current position of the read/write head and the current state as the input symbols are processed.   [6]

    (b)   Explain what this Turing machine does.   [1]

    (c)   Explain what a Universal Turing machine is.   [2]

    AQA Unit 3 Qu 11 June 2011

Chapter 54 – Backus-Naur Form

Objectives

- Explain why BNF can represent some languages that cannot be represented using regular expressions
- Use Backus-Naur Form (BNF) to represent language syntax and formulate simple production rules
- Draw a syntax diagram to represent a BNF expression

Meta-languages

In order for a computer language such as Python or Pascal to be translated into machine code, all the rules of the language must be defined unambiguously. Languages such as English, Spanish and Arabic are not at all precise, which is one reason why it is hard to get computers to understand 'natural language'.

> **Q1:** What are the possible meanings of each of the following sentences?
>
> Peter and Anna are married.
>
> A salesman visited every house in the area.
>
> Look at that dog with one eye.

Not only is English too imprecise to be used as a computer language, it is not even suitable for defining unambiguously the syntax or grammar of a computer language.

9-54

Defining the syntax of a language

In Chapter 52 we saw that regular expressions can be used to describe simple 'languages' and to match patterns in text by specifying sets of strings that satisfy given conditions.

In computer science, the syntax of a language is defined as the set of rules that define what constitutes a valid statement. It would be possible, but lengthy and time-consuming, to define a valid identifier in a given programming language using a regular expression. However, some programming language constructs involving, for example, nested brackets, cannot be defined in this way.

For this reason, special languages called **meta-languages** have been devised, and **Backus-Naur Form** (named after its two originators) is an example of one such meta-language. Many constructs that could be written using a regular expression can be expressed more succinctly using BNF.

Backus-Naur form (BNF)

The structure of BNF is composed of a list of statements of the form

LHS ::= RHS   where ::= is interpreted as 'is defined by'.

::= is known as a **meta-symbol**.

Example: <point> ::= .

<point> is called a **meta-component**, or sometimes a **syntactic variable**, and is distinguished by being enclosed in angle brackets.

The other important meta-symbol is | which means 'or'.

Thus, for example, **<digit>** can be defined as

<digit> ::= 0|1|2|3|4|5|6|7|8|9

Example1

Write the BNF definition of a variable name which, in a certain computer language, may consist of a single letter or a letter followed by a digit.

<variable name> ::= <letter>|<letter><digit>

<letter> ::= A|B|C|D|E|F|G|H|I|J|K|L|M|N|O|P|Q|R|S|T|U|V|W|X|Y|Z

<digit> ::= 0|1|2|3|4|5|6|7|8|9

Each of these individual rules is known as a **production**.

Using recursion in a BNF definition

BNF often makes use of recursion, where a statement is defined in terms of itself. e.g.

<variable list> ::= <variable>|<variable>, <variable list>

Using this definition, is A, B, C a variable list? We can show that it is, using the following reasoning:

C is a <variable>, and is therefore a <variable list>.

B is a <variable>, therefore B,C is <variable>,<variable list>, i.e. a <variable list>

A,B,C is <variable>,<variable list>

Therefore, A, B, C is a <variable list>

> **Q2:** Write the definition of a positive integer in BNF. (A positive integer must start with a digit 1-9.)
>
> **Q3:** The syntax of a real number in Pascal is defined as one or more digits, followed by a decimal point, followed by one or more digits. Write this definition using BNF.

9-54

The process of ascertaining whether a given statement is valid, given the BNF definition, is called **parsing**. The procedure is to work from left to right, replacing meta-variables with more comprehensive meta-variables at each stage.

Example 2

The following production rules have been used to define the syntax of a valid mathematical expression in a particular programming language.

<expression> ::= <factor>|<factor> * <factor>|<factor> / <factor>

<factor> ::= <term>|<term> + <term>|<term> - <term>

<term> ::= <expression>|<number>

<number> ::= <digit>|<digit><number>

<digit> ::= 0|1|2|3|4|5|6|7|8|9

Show, using these production rules, that 4 + 75 * 3 is a valid expression.

Answer

4 is a <digit>, therefore a <number>, therefore a <term>

75 is <digit><number> and is therefore a <number>, therefore a <term>

4 + 75 is a <term> + <term> therefore a <factor>

3 is a <digit>, therefore a <number>, therefore a <term>, therefore a <factor>

4 + 75 * 3 is a <factor> * <factor> and therefore an <expression>

Q4: An arithmetic expression is defined in BNF as follows:

<expression> ::= <term>|<expression> + <term>|<expression> - <term>

<term> ::= <variable>|<term> * <variable>|<term> / <variable>

<variable> ::= a|b|c|d

(a)   Show that a - b is a syntactically correct expression in this language.

(b)   Show that a + b * c is also syntactically correct.

(c)   Is a * b * c syntactically correct?

When a compiler checks a statement written in a high-level language to see if it is syntactically correct, it will parse each statement in a similar manner to that shown above.

Syntax diagrams

Syntax diagrams are a graphical method of representing the syntax of a language, and map directly to BNF.

The following symbols are used:

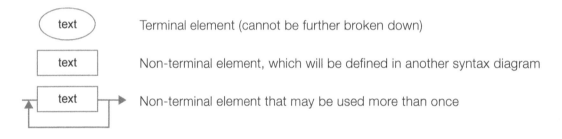

Terminal element (cannot be further broken down)

Non-terminal element, which will be defined in another syntax diagram

Non-terminal element that may be used more than once

Example 3

The syntax diagram representing a positive integer is as follows:

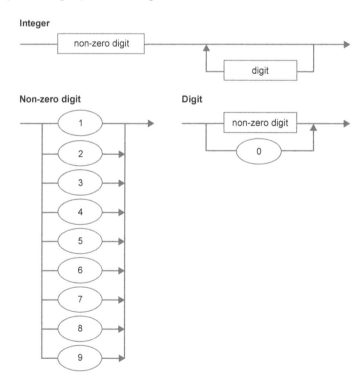

Example 4

The format of a person's initials is defined by the following syntax diagram:

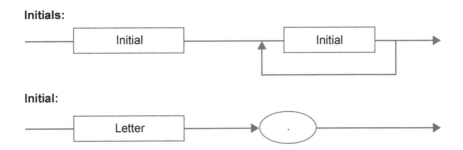

Initials:

Initial   Initial

Initial:

Letter   .

A **letter** is any alphabetic character from "A" to "Z".

(a) Write the corresponding BNF definition.

(b) Which of the following is a valid format for a person's initials?

> D.C.T.B   T.K.   W.   D.R.a.M.   A.B.C.D.

Answers

(a) <initials> ::= <initial><initial>|<initial><initials>

<initial> ::= <letter><dot>

<letter> ::= A|B|C|D|E|F|G|H|I|J|K|L|M|N|O|P|Q|R|S|T|U|V|W|X|Y|Z

<dot> ::= .

(b) T.K. and A.B.C.D. are valid initials.

Exercises

1. The following BNF definitions describe the terms **sum**, **value** and **digit**.

> <sum> ::= <value> + <value>
>
> <value> ::= <digit>|<digit><value>
>
> <digit> ::= 1|2|3|4|5|6|7|8|9|0

(a) Explain whether each of the following is a sum, a value, a digit or not defined.

    (i)   4686

    (ii)   7 + 8

    (iii)   05 + 170   [3]

(b) Write a BNF definition for **hex**, a hexadecimal number which consists of at least one digit, one letter or a mixture of digits and letters. Your definition must use digit, letter and hex only.

For example, 5, A, 2B8, FFFF are all valid examples of **hex**.   [3]

(c) The definition for **value** is

> <value> ::= <digit>|<digit><value>

Draw a syntax diagram to show the definition of **value**.

You may assume that the correct syntax diagram for **digit** already exists.   [2]

9-54

2. A vowel-string in a high-level programming language has its syntax described in BNF as follows:

    <vowel-string> ::= <vowel>|a<vowel>a|e<vowel>e|i<vowel>i|o<vowel>o|u<vowel>u

    vowel ::= a|e|i|o|u

(a) State, with reasons, whether each of the following character strings is a valid vowel-string.

    aea   uuu   AEA   aeae   sds   oooaeio

(b) The word **level** is palindromic because its letters in reverse order give the same word.

    Make simple changes to the rules given above so that a vowel-string of any length is valid if and only if it is palindromic.   [5]

3. The following BNF definition describes a registration number.

    <reg-no> ::= <code><space><number>

    <number> ::= <pos digit><digit><digit>|<pos digit><digit><digit><digit>

    <pos digit> ::= 1|2|3|4|5|6|7|8|9

    <digit> ::= 0|<pos digit>

    <code> ::= AX|AC|BB

    <space> ::= ' '

State, with reasons, whether each of the following is a valid or invalid registration number.

    AC 234   AB 13   AX 099   BB 2345   AX 6   [5]

9-54

Chapter 55 – Reverse Polish notation

Objectives

- Convert simple expressions in infix form to Reverse Polish notation (RPN) and vice versa
- Be aware of why and where RPN is used

Reverse Polish notation

Reverse Polish (also called **postfix**) notation was developed by a Pole called Jan Lukasiewicz. It is a method of writing arithmetic expressions that is particularly suited to computerised methods of evaluation. It has the following advantages and uses:

- It eliminates the need for brackets in sub-expressions
- It produces expressions in a form suitable for evaluation using a stack
- It is used in interpreters based on a stack; for example, Postscript and bytecode

The way in which we normally write arithmetic expressions is called **infix** notation, and it is not easy for a computer to evaluate such an expression directly. Consider for example the expression

    (a + b) * c

The sequence of instructions needed to evaluate this is

1. get a
2. get b
3. add them together and store the intermediate result
4. get c
5. multiply by the result of step 3.

In other words, the computer really needs the operands (a, b and c) and operators in the sequence

    a b + c *

> **Q1:** What would be the sequence of instructions needed to evaluate the expression b * c?
>
> **Q2:** What would be the sequence of instructions needed to evaluate the expression b * (c + d)?

In reverse Polish notation, the operator follows the operands – which is the logical sequence, if you are a computer.

Precedence rules

In order to translate from infix to Reverse Polish notation, we need to define the order of precedence of operators. This is shown below, in increasing order of precedence.

```
=
(
+ - )
* /
```
$\wedge$ (exponentiation, where 3^2 means 3^2)

$\sim$ (unary minus, as in -3 + 2)

9-55

Infix and postfix expressions

An expression such as (6 * 7) + 4 is known as an **infix** expression, because the operator is written between the operands.

The equivalent Reverse Polish form, 6 7 * 4 + is known as a **postfix** expression, as the operator follows the operands.

Translation from infix to Reverse Polish

A computer will use a fairly complex algorithm using a stack to translate from infix to reverse Polish notation. However, it is quite simple to do it manually with the benefit of common sense, a knowledge of the rules of precedence and a few simple rules, given below:

1. Starting from the left-hand side of the expression, allocate numbers 1, 2, 3 ... to operands and operators as follows:

   - If the next symbol is an operand, allocate the next number (1, 2, 3...) to it. If it is an operator, move to the next operand.

   - Ignore parentheses except in so far as they affect the order of calculation.

   - Bearing in mind the rules of precedence, decide which is the next operation that should be performed, and as soon as its operands have been allocated numbers, back up and allocate it the next number.

   e.g.   a + b * c

        1 5 2 4 3

        a + b * c

   Working from the left, allocate 1 to a, 2 to b. Multiplication is done before addition, so keep going and allocate 3 to c. Then back up and allocate 4 to *, and finally 5 to +.

2. Write down the tokens (operators and operands) in the order of the numbers you have allocated.

   The Reverse Polish Form of the expression is a b c * +

Example 1

Convert the following expression to Reverse Polish notation: 8 + ((7 + 1) * 2) – 6

Following the rules above, taking into account order of precedence and brackets where they affect this:

    1 7   2 4 3   6 5   9 8

    8 + ((7 + 1) * 2) - 6

Note that taking the brackets into account, 7 + 1 is the first thing to be calculated, and then this is multiplied by 2. Keep backing up every time you have one or two operands which need to be evaluated next.

The Reverse Polish Form of the expression is 8 7 1 + 2 * + 6 -

Q3: Translate into Reverse Polish Notation:

     (a)   (a + b) - x ^ y * 3

     (b)   x = - a + (c - d) / e

Translation from Reverse Polish to infix

To translate from RPN to infix, we need to perform this process in reverse.

Example 2

Convert the following RPN expression to infix notation: 25 16 18 + * 12 -

Visually scan the operands, writing them down until you find two operands followed by an operator. The unpaired operand, 25 is written down.

Bracket the next two operands with the operator between them and add them to the expression that is building up. We now have 25   (16 + 18)

Continue writing down operands until you find the next operator, which will operate on the two preceding operands, in this case * operates on 25 and (16 + 18). This gives us 25 * (16 + 18)

The next symbol is an operand, so the following operator will operate on the two operands

25 * (16 + 18) and 12, giving the final result: 25 * (16 + 18) – 12

> **Q4:** Convert the following expression from postfix (Reverse Polish) notation to infix notation.
>
> 6 3 + 7 2 – *

Evaluation of Reverse Polish notation expressions using a stack

Once a compiler has translated an arithmetic expression into reverse Polish notation, each symbol in the expression may be held in a string or array. The expression may then be evaluated using a stack, scanning the elements of the string (or array) from left to right as follows:

- If the next token is an operand, place it on the stack
- If the next token is an operator, remove the required number of operands from the stack, (two except in the case of a unary minus or exponentiation), perform the operation, and put the result on the stack.

Example 3

Convert the following expression to Reverse Polish notation, and show how the resulting expression may be evaluated using a stack.

(7 + 10 / 5) + (6 * 2)

First convert to Reverse Polish:

$$1 \quad 5 \quad 2 \quad 4 \quad 3 \qquad 9 \qquad 6 \quad 8 \quad 7$$

(7   +   10 /   5   )   +   (6   *   2   )

i.e. 7 10 5 / + 6 2 * + in Reverse Polish notation

Using a stack to evaluate the expression, the contents of the stack will change as follows:

		5				2		
	10	10	2		6	6	12	
7	7	7	7	9	9	9	9	21

> **Q5:** Convert the expression (5 + 9) / 2 – (2 * 3) to Reverse Polish notation and show how it may be evaluated using a stack.

A binary expression tree

A binary tree can be constructed to represent the expression (7 + 10 / 5) + (6 * 2) as follows:

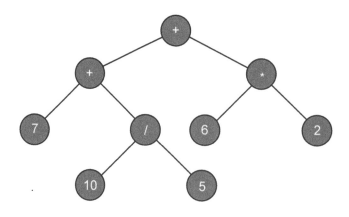

An **in-order traversal** of the tree will give the corresponding algebraic expression in **infix** format.

The nodes are visited in the sequence: 7 + 10 / 5 + 6 * 2

A **post-order traversal** of the tree will give the algebraic expression in **postfix** (reverse Polish) format.

The nodes are visited in the sequence: 7 10 5 / + 6 2 * +

> **Q6:** Draw a binary tree representing the infix expression (a + b) * (c – d)
>
> What is the result of performing a post-order traversal of the tree?

Exercises

1. At an intermediate stage of compilation, the compiler holds the following expression in reverse Polish form.

   a b * c d - - e + f g * /

   (a) Write down the original infix expression which was translated into this form. [3]

   (b) Why is reverse Polish used as an intermediate stage during compilation? [3]

2. (a) The following binary tree represents an algebraic expression. Write down the results of performing

   (i) an in-order tree traversal [2]

   (ii) a post-order tree traversal [2]

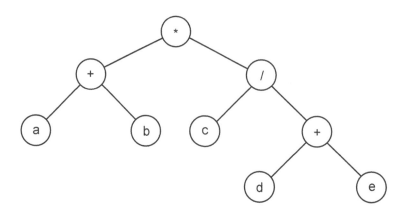

   (b) What names are given to each of these representations of the expression? [2]

Section 10

The Internet

In this section:

10

Chapter 56 – Structure of the Internet

Objectives

- Understand the structure of the Internet

- Describe the term 'Uniform Resource Locator' in the context of networking

- Explain the terms 'domain name' and 'IP address'

- Describe how domain names are organised

- Understand the purpose and function of the Domain Name Server (DNS) system

- Explain the service provided by Internet registries and why they are needed

A short history of the Internet and the World Wide Web

The Internet is a network of networks set up to allow computers to communicate with each other globally. A United States defence project in the 1960s (ARPA) created **ARPANET** to enable distant departments working on the same project to communicate without the need for physical travel. The project developed, as did their means of communication and the Internet idea was born, albeit in its infancy. In 1995 the Internet became a public hit when the World Wide Web emerged and user numbers began to climb, reaching roughly 2.5 billion users worldwide in 2015 – roughly one third of the world's population. The **World Wide Web** (WWW) is a collection of web pages that reside on computers connected to the Internet. It uses the Internet as a service to communicate the information contained within these pages. The concept of the WWW and using a browser to search the information contained within it was first developed by **Sir Tim Berners-Lee**, a British scientist working at CERN in Geneva, Switzerland. The World Wide Web is not the same as the Internet and even today, the Internet is frequently used without using the WWW.

10-56

> **Q1:** Give one example of where the Internet can be used without the World Wide Web.

Global Internet users (1995 - 2015)

▬ Internet users (Millions)   ▬▬ Percentage of the world's population

Year	Internet users (Millions)	Percentage of world's population
1995	16	0.4%
2000	361	5.8%
2005	1018	15.7%
2010	2040	28.1%
2015	2500	33%

The physical structure of the Internet

Each continent uses backbone cables connected by trans-continental leased lines fed across the sea beds. National **Internet Service Providers** (ISPs) connect directly to this backbone and distribute the Internet connection to smaller providers who in turn provide access to individual homes and businesses.

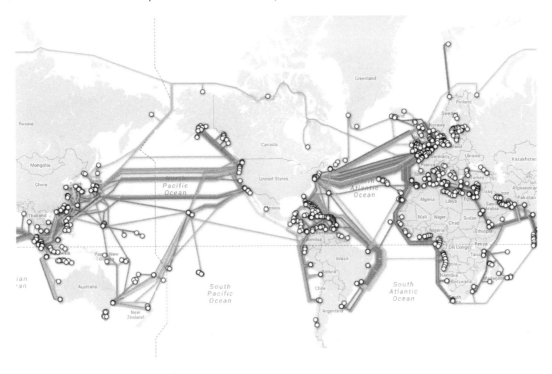

Trans-continental Internet connections, TeleGeography

10-56

Uniform Resource Locators (URLs)

A **Uniform Resource Locator** is the full address for an Internet resource. It specifies the location of a resource on the Internet, including the name and usually the file type, so that a browser can go and request it from the website server.

Internet registries and registrars

Internet registrars are needed to ensure that a particular domain name is only used by one organisation, and they hold records of all existing website names and the details of those domains that are currently available to purchase. These are companies that act as resellers for domain names and allow people and companies to purchase them. All registrars must be accredited by their governing registry.

Internet registries are five global organisations governed by the **Internet Corporation for Assigned Names and Numbers** (ICANN) with worldwide databases that hold records of all the domain names currently issued to individuals and companies, and their details. These details include the registrant's name, type (company or individual), registered mailing address, the registrar that sold the domain name and the date of registry. The registries also allocate IP addresses and keep track of which address(es) a domain name is associated with as part of the **Domain Name System** (DNS).

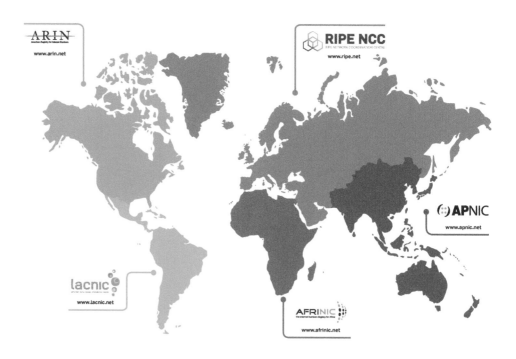

10-56

The five global Internet Registries

Domain names and the Domain Name System (DNS)

A domain name identifies the area or domain that an Internet resource resides in. These are structured into a hierarchy of smaller domains and written as a string separated by full stops as dictated by the rules of the **Domain Name System** (DNS).

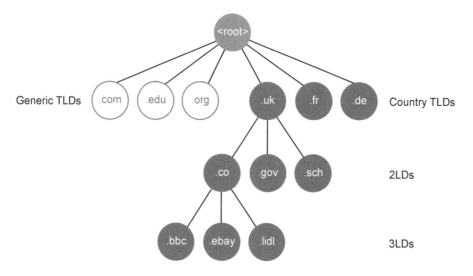

Each domain name has one or more equivalent **IP addresses**. The DNS catalogues all domain names and IP addresses in a series of global directories that domain name servers can access in order to find the correct IP address location for a resource. When a webpage is requested using the URL a user enters, the browser requests the corresponding IP address from a local DNS. If that DNS does not have the correct IP address, the search is extended up the hierarchy to another larger DNS database. The IP address is located and a data request is sent by the user's computer to that location to find the web page data. A webpage can be accessed within a browser by entering the IP address if it is known. Try entering 74.125.227.176 into a browser.

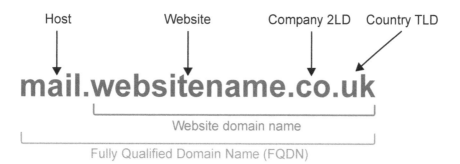

Host   Website   Company 2LD   Country TLD

mail.websitename.co.uk

Website domain name

Fully Qualified Domain Name (FQDN)

Q2: Why are IP addresses not used to access websites instead of alphanumeric addresses?

Fully Qualified Domain Names (FQDN)

A **fully qualified domain name** is one that includes the host server name, for example **www**, **mail** or **ftp** depending on whether the resource being requested is hosted on a web, mail or ftp server. This would be written as **www**.websitename.co.uk or **mail**.websitename.co.uk for example.

10-56

IP addresses

An IP or **Internet Protocol** address is a unique address that is assigned to a network device. An IP address performs a similar function to a home mailing address.

130.142.37.108

The **IP address** indicates where a packet of data is to be sent or has been sent from. **Routers** can use this address to direct the data **packet** accordingly. If a domain name is associated with a specific IP address, the IP address is the address of the server that the website resides on.

Exercises

1. A Uniform Resource Locator (URL) is the address of a resource on the Internet. For example, http:// www.pgonline.co.uk/courses/alevel/computing_test.html.

   Explain the different parts of the address.

   (a) www.   [1]

   (b) pgonline.co.uk   [1]

   (c) /courses/alevel/computing_test.html   [1]

2. A village hall committee is considering purchasing a lease on a web domain to set up a new website to advertise their events. They have been advised to contact an Internet registrar.

   (a) Explain the role of an Internet registrar.   [3]

   (b) What is the primary role of an Internet Service Provider (ISP)?   [1]

Chapter 57 – Packet switching and routers

Objectives

- Understand the role of packet switching and routers

- Know the main components of a packet

- Consider where and why routers and gateways are used

- Explain how routing is achieved across the Internet

Packet switching

Packet switching is a method of communicating packets of data across a network on which other similar communications are happening simultaneously. The communications cables are shared between many communications to allow efficient use of them, in contrast to the older circuit-switched telephone network which allowed only one two-way communication at a time along a single cable. Website data that you receive arrives as a series of packets and an email will leave you in a series of packets.

Data packets

Data that is to be transmitted across a network is broken down in more manageable chunks called **packets**. The size of each packet in a transmission can be fixed or variable, but most are between 500 and 1500 bytes. Each packet contains a **header** and a **payload** containing the body of data being sent. Some packets may also use a trailer section with a **checksum** or **Cyclical Redundancy Check** (CRC) to detect transmission errors by creating and attaching a hash total calculated from the data contained in the packets. The CRC checksum is recalculated for each packet upon receipt and a match is used to help verify that the payload data has not changed during transmission. If the CRC totals differ, the packet is refused with suspected data corruption and a new copy is requested from the sender.

The header (much like the box(es) of a consignment you might send or receive through the post) includes the sender's and the recipient's IP addresses, the protocol being used with this type of packet and the number of the packet in the sequence being sent, e.g. packet 1 of 8. They also include the **Time To Live** (TTL) or **hop limit**, after which point the data packet expires and is discarded.

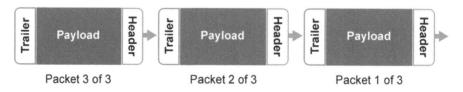

Packet 3 of 3   Packet 2 of 3   Packet 1 of 3

Data packets queueing to be sent

Q1: Why is the sender's IP address included in the packet header?

The payload of the packet contains the actual data being sent. Upon receipt, the packets are reassembled in the correct order and the data is extracted.

Routing packets across the Internet

The success of packet switching relies on the ability of packets to be sent from sender to recipient along entirely separate routes from each other. At the moment that a packet leaves the sender's computer, the fastest or least congested route is taken to the recipient's computer. They can be easily reassembled in the correct order at the receiving end and any packets that don't make it can be requested again.

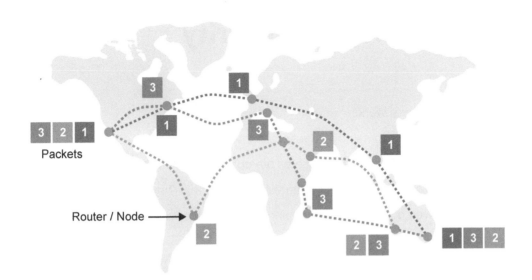

Packets

Router / Node ⟶

Q2: What information is included in the packet header to enable the receiving computer to reassemble packets in the correct order?

Routers

Each node in the diagram above represents a **router**. Routers are used to connect at least two networks, commonly two LANs or WANs, or to connect a LAN and its ISP's network. The act of traversing a router from one network to another is referred to as a **hop**. The job of a router is to read the recipient's IP address in each packet and forward it on to the recipient via the fastest and least congested route to the next router, which will do the same until the packet reaches its destination. Routers use routing tables to store and update the locations of other network devices and the most efficient routes to them. A routing algorithm is used to find the optimum route. The routing algorithm used to decide the best route can become a bottleneck in network traffic since the decision making process can be complicated. A common shortest path algorithm used in routing is **Dijkstra's algorithm**. (See Chapter 48.)

When a router is connected to the Internet, the IP address of the port connecting it must be registered with the Internet registry because this IP address must be unique over the whole Internet.

10-57

Gateways

Routing packets from one network to another requires a router if the networks share the same protocols, for example TCP/IP. Where these protocols differ between networks, a **gateway** is used rather than a router to translate between them. All of the header data is stripped from the packet leaving only the raw data and new header data is added in the format of the new network before the gateway sends the packet on its way again. Gateways otherwise perform a similar job to routers in moving data packets towards their destination.

Exercises

1. Major parts of the Internet run on a packet switched network that relies on routers and gateways to communicate.

   (a)   What is meant by the term packet switching? [2]

   (b)   A data packet contains a header and a payload. The header contains data that it used to route the packet to its destination.

       State three data items that might be contained in a data packet's header. [3]

   (c)   Explain the difference between a router and a gateway. [2]

Chapter 58 – Internet security

Objectives

- Understand how a firewall works
- Explain symmetric and asymmetric encryption and key exchange
- Explain how digital signatures and certificates are obtained and used
- Discuss worms, Trojans and viruses and the vulnerabilities that they exploit
- Discuss how improved code quality, monitoring and protection can be used against such threats

Firewalls

A **Firewall** is a security checkpoint designed to prevent unauthorised access between two networks, usually an internal trusted network and an external, deemed untrusted, network; often the Internet. Firewalls can be implemented in both hardware and/or software. A router may contain a firewall.

A typical firewall consists of a separate computer containing two **Network Interface Cards** (NICs), with one connected to the internal network, and the other connected to the external network. Using special firewall software, each data packet that attempts to pass between the two NICs is analysed against preconfigured rules (**packet filters**), then accepted or rejected. A firewall may also act as a **proxy server**.

Packet filtering

10-58

Packet filtering, also referred to as **static filtering**, controls network access according to network administrator rules and policies by examining the source and destination IP addresses in packet headers. If the IP addresses match those recorded on the administrator's 'permitted' list, they are accepted. Static filtering can also block packets based on the protocols being used and the port numbers they are trying to access. A **port** is similar to an airport gate, where an incoming aircraft reaches the correct airport (the computer or network at a particular IP address) and is directed to a particular gate to allow passengers into the airport, or in this case to download the packet's payload data to the computer.

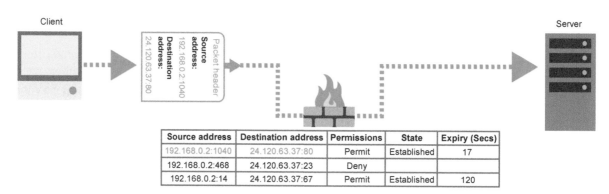

Source address	Destination address	Permissions	State	Expiry (Secs)
192.168.0.2:1040	24.120.63.37:80	Permit	Established	17
192.168.0.2:468	24.120.63.37:23	Deny		
192.168.0.2:14	24.120.63.37:67	Permit	Established	120

Certain protocols use particular ports. Telnet, for example, is used to remotely access computers and uses port 23. If Telnet is disallowed by a network administrator, any packets attempting to connect through port 23 will be dropped or rejected to deny access. A dropped packet is quietly removed, whereas a rejected packet will cause a rejection notice to be sent back to the sender.

Stateful inspection

Rather than relying on the IP addresses, protocols and port numbers to govern a packet's safe passage, **stateful inspection** or **dynamic filtering** can also examine the payload contents of a data packet to better assess it for safety. It can also create temporary contextual rules based on the passage of previous packets in a 'conversation'. This is to ensure that incoming responses (to your outgoing packets) arriving through the same port numbers, and with the same IP addresses, can be temporarily allowed during that communication stream. Routers usually keep the 'conversation' data in a Connection Table which is dynamically updated and referred to in conjunction with rules created by administrators of the network. An example of this would be when a browser makes a request to a specific web server for a web page. The packets containing the web page data returning from the web server would be allowed since the dynamic filter knows that these are in response to the recent request. This provides an added security measure against port scanning for covert access to a computer, since ports are closed off until connection to the specific port is requested by a computer on the protected side of the firewall.

Proxy servers

A **proxy server** intercepts all packets entering and leaving a network, hiding the true network addresses of the source from the recipient. This enables privacy and anonymous surfing. A proxy can also maintain a cache of websites commonly visited and return the web page data to the user immediately without the need to reconnect to the Internet and re-request the page from the website server. This speeds up user access to web page data and reduces web traffic. If a web page is not in the cache, then the proxy will make a request of its own on behalf of the user to the web server using its own IP address and forward the returned data to the user, adding the page to its cache for other users going through the same proxy server to access. A proxy server may serve hundreds, if not thousands of users.

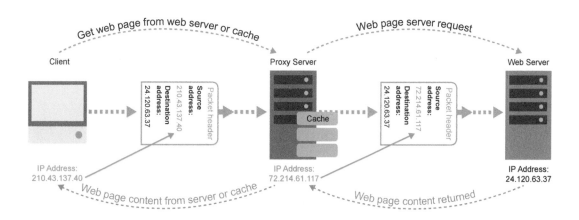

Proxy servers are often used to filter requests providing administrative control over the content that users may demand. A common example is a school web-proxy that filters undesirable or potentially unsafe online content in accordance with their school usage policies. Such proxies may also log user data with their requests.

Encryption

Encryption is the process of scrambling data so that it becomes very difficult to unscramble and interpret without the correct key. Encrypted data is known as **ciphertext**, and the original interpretable data is known as **plaintext**. The process of encryption is carried out using a cryptographic algorithm and a key.

10-58

Symmetric (Private key) encryption

Symmetric encryption, also known as **private key** encryption, uses the same key to encrypt and decrypt data. This means that the key must also be transferred (known as **key exchange**) to the same destination as the ciphertext which causes obvious security problems. The key can be intercepted as easily as the ciphertext message to decrypt the data. For this reason **asymmetric** encryption can be used instead.

Q1: What are the risks associated with using private key encryption?

Asymmetric (Public key) encryption

Asymmetric encryption uses two separate, but related keys. One key, known as the **public key**, is made public so that others wishing to send you data can use this to encrypt the data. This public key cannot decrypt data. Another **private key** is known only by you and only this can be used to decrypt the data. It is virtually impossible to deduce the private key from the public key. It is possible that a message could be encrypted using your own public key and sent to you by a malicious third party impersonating a trusted individual. To prevent this, a message can be digitally 'signed' to authenticate the sender.

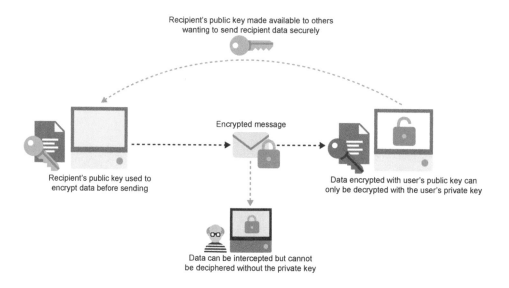

Recipient's public key made available to others wanting to send recipient data securely

Encrypted message

Recipient's public key used to encrypt data before sending

Data encrypted with user's public key can only be decrypted with the user's private key

Data can be intercepted but cannot be deciphered without the private key

Q2: Governments sometimes demand copies of encryption keys in order to decrypt messages if necessary. What reasons are there for and against governments doing this?

Digital signatures

A **digital signature** is the equivalent of a handwritten signature or security stamp, but offers even greater security. First of all, a mathematical value is calculated from the unencrypted message data. This value is also referred to as a **hash total**, **checksum** or **digest**. Since the hash total is generated from the entire message, even the slightest change in the message will produce a different total. The sender of the message uses their own **private key** to encrypt the hash total. The encrypted total becomes the digital signature since only the holder of the private key could have encrypted it. The signature is attached to the message to be sent and the whole message including the digital signature is encrypted using the recipient's **public key** before being sent. The recipient then decrypts the message using their private key, and decrypts the digital signature using the sender's public key. The hash total is then reproduced based on the message data and if this matches the total in the digital signature, it is certain that the message genuinely came from the sender and that no parts of the message were changed during transmission.

10-58

To ensure that the message could not be copied and resent at a later date, the time and date can be included in the original message, which if altered, would cause a different hash total to be generated.

Digital signatures can be used with any kind of message regardless of whether encryption has also been used. They can be used with most email clients or browsers making it easy to sign outgoing communication and validate signed incoming messages. If set up to use digital signatures, your browser should warn you if you download something that does not have a digital signature. This would also mean that anything sent by you including online commercial and banking transactions can be verified as your own.

Q3: Assuming their private key has not been compromised, a digital signature authenticates the sender beyond legal doubt. How might this help protect against viruses?

Hoax digital signatures could be created using a bogus private key claiming to be that of a trusted individual. In order to mitigate against this, a **digital certificate** verifies that a sender's public key is formally registered to that particular sender.

Digital certificates

While digital signatures verify the trustworthiness of message content, a **digital certificate** is issued by official **Certificate Authorities** (CAs) such as Symantec or Verisign and verifies the trustworthiness of a message sender or website. This certificate allows the holder to use the **Public Key Infrastructure** or PKI. The certificate contains the certificate's serial number, the expiry date, the name of the holder, a copy of their public key, and the digital signature of the CA so that the recipient can authenticate the certificate as real. Digital certificates operate within the Transport layer of the TCP/IP protocol stack using TLS (Transport Layer Security), which is beginning to supersede SSL (Secure Sockets Layer) security. TCP/IP is covered in more detail in the following chapter.

10-58

Worms, Trojans and viruses

Worms, Trojans and viruses are all types of **malware** or **malicious software**. They are all designed to cause inconvenience, loss or damage to programs, data or computer systems.

Viruses and worm subclasses

Viruses and **worms** have the ability to self-replicate by spreading copies of themselves. A worm is a sub-class of virus, but the difference between the two is that viruses rely on other host files (usually executable programs) to be opened in order to spread themselves, whereas worms do not. A worm is standalone software that can replicate itself without any user intervention. Viruses come in various types but most become memory resident when their host file is executed. Once the virus is in memory, any other uninfected file that runs becomes infected when it is copied into memory. Other common viruses reside in macro files usually attached to word processing and spreadsheet data files. When the data file is opened, the virus spreads to infect the template and subsequently other files that you create. Macro viruses are usually less harmful than other viruses but can still be very annoying.

The Cascade virus caused text characters to fall from the top of the screen

A worm does not generally hide itself inside another file, but will usually enter the computer through a vulnerability or by tricking the user into opening a file; often an attachment in an email. Rather than simply infecting other files like a virus on your own machine, a worm can replicate itself and send copies to other users from your computer; commonly by emailing others in your electronic address book.

Owing to the ability of a worm to copy itself, worms are often responsible for using up bandwidth, system memory or network resources, causing computers to slow and servers to stop responding.

> **Q4:** Look up the ILOVEYOU, Melissa, Blaster and Cascade viruses or worms. Why should you exercise caution in opening attachments in emails or data files containing macro code?

Trojans

A Trojan is so called after the story of the great horse of Troy, according to which soldiers hid inside a large wooden horse offered as a gift to an opposition castle. The castle guards wheeled the wooden horse inside their castle walls, and the enemy soldiers jumped out from inside the horse to attack. A Trojan is every bit as cunning and frequently manifests itself inside a seemingly useful file, game or utility that you want to install on your computer. When installed, the payload is released, often without any obvious irritation. A common use for a Trojan is to open a back door to your computer system that the Trojan creator can exploit. This can be in order to harvest your personal information, or to use your computer power and network bandwidth to send thousands of spam emails to others. Groups of Internet-enabled computers used like this are called botnets. Unlike viruses and worms, Trojans cannot self-replicate.

10-58

The Procession of the Trojan Horse in Troy - Giovanni Domenico Tiepolo, c.1760

System vulnerabilities

Malware exploits vulnerabilities in our systems, be they human error or software bugs. People may switch off their firewalls or fail to renew virus protection which will create obvious weaknesses in their systems. Administrative rights can also fail to prevent access to certain file areas which may otherwise be breached by viral threats. Otherwise cracks in software where data is passed from one function, module or application to another (which is often deemed to have been checked and trusted somehow by the source) may open opportunities for attackers.

Protection against viral threats

Code quality is a primary vulnerability of systems. Many malware attacks exploit a phenomenon called 'buffer overflow' which normally occurs when a program accidentally writes values to memory locations too small to handle them, and inadvertently overwrites the values in neighbouring locations that it is not supposed to have access to. As a result of a buffer overflow attack, overflow data is often interpreted as instructions. The virus could be written to take advantage of this by forcing the program to write something to memory which may consequently alter its behaviour in a way that benefits the attacker.

Social engineering, including phishing, is a confidence trick used to persuade individuals to open files, Internet links and emails containing malware. Spam filtering and education in the use of caution is the most effective method against this sort of vulnerability.

Regular operating system and antivirus software updates will also help to reduce the risk of attack. Virus checkers usually scan for all other malware types and not just viruses, and since new variants are created all the time to exploit vulnerabilities in systems software, it is vital that your system has the latest protection. In the worst cases, a lack of monitoring and protection within a company can make national headlines.

Exercises

1. Software is being developed to allow secure transmission of data over the Internet.

   The two computers involved in a communication will be known as A and B.

   (a) What is *encryption*?   [1]

   (b) The data being transmitted will be encrypted using public and private keys. A and B will each have a public key and a private key.

   A will encrypt the data that it is sending using B's public key.

   Explain why the data should not be encrypted using:

   (i) A's public key   [1]

   (ii) A's private key   [1]

   (c) The communication will be made more secure by the use of a digital signature attached to the end of the message.

   - State the purpose of a digital signature

   - Explain how it will be created and used in the data transmissions process from A to B.

   In your answer you will be assessed on your ability to use good English, and to organise your answer clearly in complete sentences, using specialist vocabulary where appropriate.   [6]

   AQA Unit 3 Qu 5 Jun 2012

2. Malicious attacks on systems are frequently identified and blocked by various systems.

   (a) How might a proxy server reduce the risks of malware attacks on a network?   [1]

   (b) Explain how stateful inspection provides greater security against port scanning than simple packet filtering   [1]

   (c) Give **three** methods that school systems administrators can use to reduce the threat of malware.   [3]

10-58

Chapter 59 – TCP/IP, standard application layer protocols

Objectives

- Describe the roles of the four layers in the TCP/IP protocol stack

- Describe the role of sockets in the TCP/IP stack

- Be familiar with MAC addresses

- Explain and differentiate between the common protocols and the well-known ports they use

- Be familiar with transferring files using FTP as an anonymous and non-anonymous user

- Know how Secure Shell (SSH) is used for remote management including the use of application level protocols for sending and retrieving email

- Explain the role of an email server in sending and retrieving email

- Explain the role of a web server in serving up web pages in text form

- Understand the role of a web browser in retrieving web pages and web page resources and rendering these accordingly

The TCP/IP protocol stack

10-59

The **Transmission Control Protocol / Internet Protocol (TCP/IP)** protocol stack is set of networking protocols that work together as four connected layers, passing incoming and outgoing data packets up and down the layers during network communication. The four layers are the:

- Application layer

- Transport layer

- Network layer

- Link layer

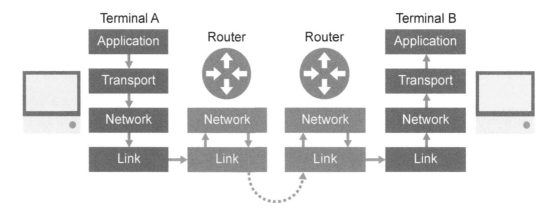

Figure 59.1

The role of the four layers in the stack

Various protocols operate at each layer of the stack, each with different roles. In each layer, the data to be sent is wrapped, or encapsulated in an envelope containing new packet data as it descends the layers and is unwrapped again at the receiving end in a networking equivalent of a game of pass the parcel.

The application layer

The **application layer** sits at the top of the stack and uses protocols relating to the application being used to transmit data over a network, usually the Internet. If this application is a browser, for example, it would select an appropriate higher-level protocol for the communication such as HTTP, POP3 or FTP.

Imagine the following text data is to be sent via a browser using the **Hypertext Transfer Protocol** (HTTP):

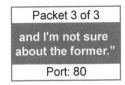

> "Only two things are infinite, the universe and human stupidity, and I'm not sure about the former."
> *Albert Einstein*

The transport layer

The **transport layer** uses the **Transmission Control Protocol (TCP)** to establish an **end-to-end connection** with the recipient computer. The data is then split into packets and labelled with the packet number, the total number of packets and the **port** number through which the packet should route. This ensures it is handled by the correct application on the recipient computer. In the example below, port 80 is used as this is a common port used by the HTTP protocol, called upon by the destination browser.

If any packets go astray during the connection, the transport layer requests retransmission of lost packets. Receipt of packets is also acknowledged.

Packet 1 of 3	Packet 2 of 3	Packet 3 of 3
"Only two things are infinite,	the universe and human stupidity,	and I'm not sure about the former."
Port: 80	Port: 80	Port: 80

The network layer

The **network layer**, sometimes referred to as the **IP layer** or **Internet layer**, adds the source and destination **IP addresses. Routers** operate on the network layer and will use these IP addresses to forward the packets on to the destination. The addition of an **IP address** to the **port** number forms a **socket**, e.g. 42.205.110.140:80, in the same way that the addition of a person's name is added to a street address on an envelope in order to direct the letter to the correct person within a building. A socket specifies which device the packet must be sent to and the application being used on that device.

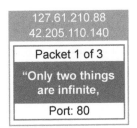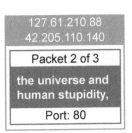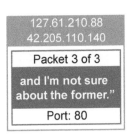

127.61.210.88 42.205.110.140	127.61.210.88 42.205.110.140	127.61.210.88 42.205.110.140
Packet 1 of 3	Packet 2 of 3	Packet 3 of 3
"Only two things are infinite,	the universe and human stupidity,	and I'm not sure about the former."
Port: 80	Port: 80	Port: 80

The link layer

The link layer is the physical connection between network nodes and adds the unique **Media Access Control (MAC)** addresses identifying the **Network Interface Cards (NICs)** of the source and destination devices. These means that once the packet finds the correct network using the IP address, it can then locate the correct piece of hardware. MAC addresses are changed at each hop, the source MAC address being the address of the device sending the packet for that specific hop and the destination MAC address that of the device receiving the packet for that particular hop. Unless the two computers are on the same network, the destination MAC address will initially be the MAC address of the first router that the packet is sent to.

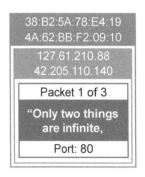
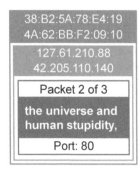
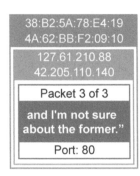

At the receiving end, the MAC address is stripped off by the link layer, which passes the packets on to the network layer. The IP addresses are then removed by the network layer which passes them on to the transport layer. The transport layer uses the port number to determine which application to pass the data to in the application layer, then removes the port numbers and reassembles the packets in the correct order. The resulting data is then passed to the application which presents the data for the user. Since routers operate on the network layer, source and destination MAC addresses are changed at each router node. Packets, therefore, move up and down the lower layers in the stack as they pass through each router or switch between the client and the server as shown in Figure 59.1.

> **Q1:** Imagine you are sending a friend a consignment of 5000 widgets in five boxes via a shipping agent. What information would you, the shipping agent, an intermediary depot and the delivery drivers write on the boxes or on a cover note inside? How does this relate to the TCP/IP stack?

10-59

Media Access Control (MAC) addresses

A **MAC** address is a unique 12-digit hexadecimal code that is hardcoded on every **Network Interface Card** (NIC) during manufacture. This uniquely identifies a particular printer, mobile phone, computer or router, wireless or wired, anywhere in the world so that data packets can be routed directly to them.

MAC: 00-71-5B-A9-38-4A

Well-known server ports and standard application level protocols

A **port** determines which application may deal with a data packet as it enters your computer. Several common application level **protocols** use standard ports on the server.

Server port number	Protocol
20	File Transfer Protocol (FTP) data
21	File Transfer Protocol (FTP) control instructions
22	Secure Shell (SSH) remote login
23	Telnet (unencrypted) remote login
25	Simple Mail Transfer Protocol (SMTP)
80 & 8080	Hypertext Transfer Protocol (HTTP)
110	Post Office Protocol v3 (POP3)
143	Interim Mail Access Protocol (IMAP)
443	Hypertext Transfer Protocol Secure (HTTPS)

The client port that a server request is returned to is usually a temporary and arbitrary port number. This is a security measure to ensure that hackers do not know which ports are open on a client machine.

> **Q2:** The following socket address 132.41.160.10:443 is given as the destination of a data packet. What port number is the packet using? What is a protocol? Which protocol is the packet following? What services might use such a protocol?

Transferring files with FTP

File Transfer Protocol (FTP) is a very efficient method used to transfer data across a network, often the Internet. FTP works as a high level protocol in the Application layer using a set of FTP commands. Using an FTP software client sat on top of the protocol, user actions can generate the FTP commands automatically as shown in the figure below. The user is presented with a file management screen showing the file and folder structure in both the local computer and the remote website. Files are transferred simply by dragging them from one area to the other. FTP sites may also be used by software companies offering large updates, or by press photographers to upload their latest photographs to a remote newspaper headquarters for example. Most FTP sites require a username and password to authenticate the user, but some sites could be configured to allow **anonymous use** without the need for any login information.

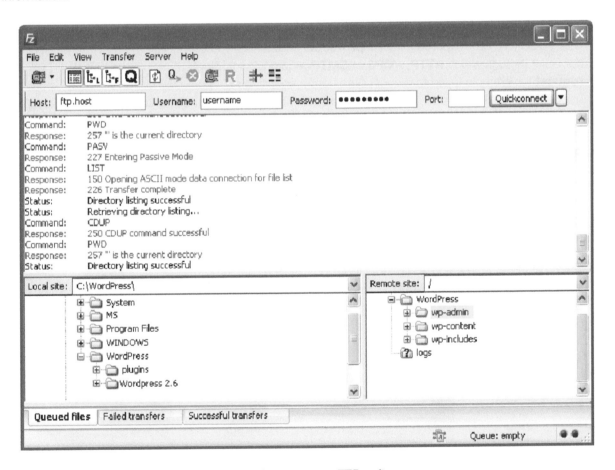

FileZilla – Open source FTP software

Common FTP Commands as shown in the figure above:

PWD Print working directory   CDUP Change to parent directory

LIST Return file or directory information   PASV Enter passive mode

10-59

Remote management using Secure Shell (SSH)

Secure Shell (SSH) is used for remotely accessing and managing a computer. It is a modern, and secure replacement of an older **Telnet** protocol which used no encryption at all. SSH uses public key encryption, requiring a digital certificate to authenticate the user. It is commonly used by network administrators to remotely manage their business servers. The commands used to control the server remotely are similar to the original MS-DOS commands used to control a PC before the Windows interface was developed. Some common commands are given below:

Command	Description
cd [folder name]	Change directory to a named folder
cd..	Move up one folder level
pwd	Print the working directory e.g. /media/images/artwork/
cp logo.png images/logo.png	Copy a file (logo.png) to a new location (/images)
cat index.html	Display the contents of a file
ls *.png	List all files with the extension .png

Q3: Compare and contrast the Telnet and SSH protocols.

Using application level protocols with SSH

Using SSH with other application level **protocols** means that you can create a 'tunnel' through port 22 (for SSH) through which **HTTP**, **POP3** or **SMTP** requests can operate. This means that an HTTP '**GET**' **request** for example (used to request data from a specified resource), can not only be sent securely using secure shell encryption, but can also bypass any network restrictions that may have been placed on other ports that might usually be associated with these services.

The role of a mail server in retrieving and sending email

A **mail server** acts as a virtual post office for all incoming and outgoing emails. These servers route mail according to its database of local network user's email addresses as it comes and goes, and store it until it can be retrieved. **Post Office Protocol (v3) (POP3)** is responsible for retrieving emails from a mail server that temporarily stores your incoming mail. When emails are retrieved, they are transferred to your local computer, be it a desktop or mobile phone, and deleted from the server. As a result, if you are using different devices to access email via POP3, you will find that they don't synchronise the same emails on each device. **Internet Message Access Protocol (IMAP)** is another email protocol that is designed to keep emails on the server, thus maintaining synchronicity between devices. **Simple Mail Transfer Protocol (SMTP)** is used to transfer outgoing emails from one server to another or from an email client to the server when sending an email.

Q4: Georgina is trying to contact her brother Nick, who is currently travelling overseas. Georgina has no idea where Nick is exactly and sends an email to his webmail account. Explain, with reference to the protocols involved, how Nick is able to pick up Georgina's message.

10-59

Web servers

A **web server** typically hosts a website and handles client requests, typically using HTTP, to send content to users wanting to view pages of the site. The web pages are stored as text files, usually written in **HTML**, **CSS** and/or **JavaScript** and sent to a browser to render them accordingly.

```
<!DOCTYPE html>                    <body>
<html>                             <div id="page">
<head>                             <h1>
   <title>Piranhas</title>            The Red-bellied Piranha
                                   </h1>
<style>                            <img src="piranha.png"
h1{color: red}                     width=600px>
</style>                           </div>
</head>                            </body>
                                   </html>
```

HTML code is stored in text form using <tags> to help browsers render the pages correctly

The server also handles traffic to and from the site and may load balance requests across several servers hosting the same website to ensure that visitors to the site all get a smooth experience without delay during times of particularly high traffic.

The role of a browser in rendering web pages

When a browser receives an HTTP response from a web server, the text document, containing the HTML (for content), CSS (for styling) and/or JavaScript (to run client-side code) for a page is parsed to break it down to fit a standard hierarchical model.

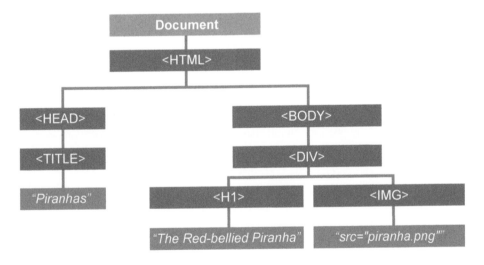

An HTML DOM tree

The HTML is first broken down into a hierarchy of tags called a **Document Object Model (DOM)** tree in order for the browser to structure the code. The styles from the CSS form their own **CSSOM (CSS Object Model)** and are related to their corresponding HTML tags. Lastly, any JavaScript is parsed and executed. Further HTTP requests are made to download other resources such as additional images or a style sheet from the server to the local machine. The browser then renders or 'paints' the page on the screen as the designer intended when the code was written.

Exercises

1. All Internet communications use the TCP/IP protocol stack, which is considered to have four layers – the application, transport, network and link layers.

Describe the roles of each layer when two devices are communicating over the Internet.

In your answer you will also be assessed on your ability to use good English, and to organise your answer clearly in complete sentences, using specialist vocabulary where appropriate. [8]

AQA Comp 2 Qu 5 Jun 2011

2. An ICT technician at a secondary school has access to a variety of programs that she uses to manage a group of web servers.

(a) State **one** use for each of the protocols listed below.

(i) Telnet [1]

(ii) FTP [1]

(iii) POP3 [1]

(b) Whilst remotely connecting to one of the servers the technician executes a command that displays the current network connections. Figure 1 shows these network connections.

```
Active Internet Connections

Proto  Recv-Q  Send-Q  Local Address        Foreign Address          (state)

tcp4   0       0       192.168.3.205:80     74.125.4.148:58539     ESTABLISHED

tcp4   0       0       192.168.3.205:80     208.43.202.29:57458    ESTABLISHED

tcp4   37      0       192.168.3.205:25     208.43.202.29:57459    CLOSE_WAIT
```

Figure 1

From Figure 1 provide an example of the following:

(i) IP address [1]

(ii) Port [1]

(iii) Socket [1]

(c) State two reasons why the technician uses remote management software from her computer rather than going to the actual servers. [2]

AQA Comp 2 Qu 3 Jun 2012

Chapter 60 – IP addresses

Objectives

- Know that an IP address is split into a network identifier and a host identifier part
- Know how a subnet mask is used to identify the network identifier part of the IP address
- Know that there are currently two standards of IP address, (v4 and v6) and why v6 was introduced
- Distinguish between routable and non-routable IP addresses
- Understand the purpose and function of the Dynamic Host Configuration Protocol (DHCP) system
- Explain the basic concepts of Network Address Translation (NAT) and port forwarding and why they are used

The IP address structure

An Internet Protocol address or **IP address** is a unique numerical address used to identify a host computer or network node trying to communicate over IP on the Internet.

IP standards

There are two standards of IP addressing currently in use. **IPv4** and **IPv6**. The IPv4 system was first deployed in 1983 providing 4 billion possible address combinations. It was inconceivable then that the world would need any more, but we are fast running out of unique addresses. In 1999, IPv6 was introduced using 128 bits expressed as a hexadecimal string rather than binary (for example, **3dfb:1730:4935:0007:0340:fe2f:fb71:48af**). IPv6 now offers 340 trillion, trillion, trillion unique addresses. That ought to be enough! It is thought that by 2020, (largely driven by the **Internet of Things**), IPv6 will become the new global standard but the inevitable changeover from IPv4 is not an entirely straightforward exercise as the two systems are incompatible with each other. This means that every IPv4 device or software application operating on the Internet will need to be upgraded or replaced.

10-60

IPv4

An IPv4 address consists of a 32-bit number written in a **dotted-decimal** notation. Each part represents an 8-bit binary pattern giving a range of 0-255 for each decimal number.

172.16.114.35

10101100 00010000 01110010 00100011

32 Bits (4 Bytes)

Reserved IP addresses

Some IP addresses cannot be used for an individual network or host.

- 127.x.x.x are private, non-routable addresses used for diagnostics within local networks only.
- x.x.x.0 is the network identifier
- x.x.x.255 is reserved as the broadcast address on that subnet where data is sent simultaneously to all subnetwork hosts
- x.x.x.1 is conventionally the default router address

Network and host identifiers

An IPv4 address contains two parts to identify both the individual network and the host computer within that network. The network part of the address uses the first bits in the 32-bit address and therefore the size of this **network ID** determines the number of bits remaining in the address for the **host ID**.

Classful addressing

Historically, a systems of classes was used to define the size or proportion of the network and host identifiers within a 32-bit IP address. Class A networks had very few network identifiers (7 bits = 128 network identifiers, less all-0 and all-1 addresses = 126 networks), each with millions of host addresses, suitable for the world's largest organisations. Conversely Class C had millions of networks with few hosts. If classful addressing is used, then the division of an IP address between host ID and network ID always happens in a small number of fixed positions. For classless addressing, the split between host ID and network ID can be made anywhere within an IP address.

Classless addressing

The more modern classless system specifies the number of bits in the subnet mask as in this example:

103.27.104.92/24

where the '/24' indicates that the first 24 bits of the IP address are the network ID and the remaining 8 are the host ID. This has the significant advantage over the classful system of allowing the split between network ID and host ID being possible anywhere within the 32 bits, e.g. 22 bits for network ID, 10 bits for host ID. This is a far more flexible arrangement which is intended to overcome the limitations of there being a very limited number of IP blocks in the classful system.

10-60

Q1: What Network ID and Host ID split might you implement for a small business with up to 25 network users and why?

Subnet masking

A **subnet mask** is used in conjunction with an IP address to identify the two unique parts of the address. A subnet mask of 255.255.255.0 indicates that 24 bits have been used for the network ID, corresponding to a suffix of '/24' in a classless IP address. This would leave 254 (1-254) unique addresses (excluding 0 and 255 which are reserved as generic and broadcast addresses) remaining for the host computers on this network. The IP address of 140.24.112.0 may be the network address, and 140.24.112.57 may identify the host computer on that network where 57 is the **host ID**. An organisation likely to require more than 254 unique addresses should use a subnet mask with a smaller **network ID**.

A subnet mask is 'ANDed' with the IP address using the bitwise logical **AND** operator to separate out the **network ID** from the full IP address.

Note that the mask is applied independently to the IP addresses of both the source and destination computers.

A computer sending data across a network will use a **subnet mask** and the destination IP address to determine from the network ID whether or not the destination computer is on the same subnetwork. This is done by performing the same AND operation between the computer's own IP address and the subnet mask; if the two network IDs produced are the same then the computers are on the same network so data can be sent directly between them. Otherwise the sending computer must send the data to a router for forwarding to the network that the destination computer is on.

	128	64	32	16	8	4	2	1		128	64	32	16	8	4	2	1		128	64	32	16	8	4	2	1		128	64	32	16	8	4	2	1
				140					.				24					.				112					.				57				
IP Address:	1	0	0	0	1	1	0	0	.	0	0	0	1	1	0	0	0	.	0	1	1	1	0	0	0	0	.	0	0	1	1	1	0	0	1
Subnet mask:	1	1	1	1	1	1	1	1	.	1	1	1	1	1	1	1	1	.	1	1	1	1	1	1	1	1	.	0	0	0	0	0	0	0	0
Network ID:	1	0	0	0	1	1	0	0	.	0	0	0	1	1	0	0	0	.	0	1	1	1	0	0	0	0	.	0	0	0	0	0	0	0	0

Subnetting

A network administrator of a large organisation using an **IP address** with a 16-bit network ID may wish to create **subnetwork** segments within their own larger IP network in order to ease management and improve efficiency by routing data through one segment only. Using a bus network, this would allow two computers in subnetwork A to communicate at the same time as two computers in subnetwork B avoiding any collisions. **Subnetting** reduces the size of the broadcast domain which can improve security, speed and reliability.

A **subnet ID** is created by using the most significant bits from the host ID section of the IP addresses. In the example below, the eight most significant bits of the 16-bit host ID have been used as a subnet ID leaving 8 bits or 254 ($28 = 254-2$ to exclude all-zero and all-one) unique host addresses in each of 256 (28) new subnetworks. The term Subnet ID is often used to cover the Network ID and Subnet ID together. For example, if you configure a computer or home router no distinction is made between the two.

10-60

	128	64	32	16	8	4	2	1		128	64	32	16	8	4	2	1		128	64	32	16	8	4	2	1		128	64	32	16	8	4	2	1
				172					.				16					.				1					.				5				
IP Address:	1	0	1	0	1	1	0	0	.	0	0	0	1	0	0	0	0	.	0	0	0	0	0	0	0	1	.	0	0	0	0	0	1	0	1
Subnet mask:	1	1	1	1	1	1	1	1	.	1	1	1	1	1	1	1	1	.	1	1	1	1	1	1	1	1	.	0	0	0	0	0	0	0	0
	1	0	1	0	1	1	0	0	.	0	0	0	1	0	0	0	0	.	0	0	0	0	0	0	0	1	.	0	0	0	0	0	0	0	0
				Network ID																	**Subnet ID**									**Host ID**					

A network diagram showing subnetwork segments might look like this:

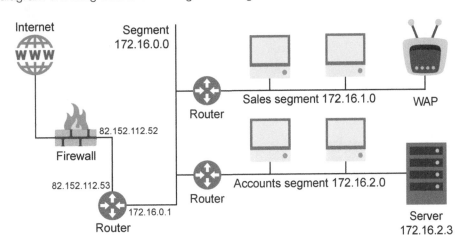

Q2: Suggest a suitable IP address for the Wireless Access Point in the diagram above.

Public and private IP addresses

A **public** (or **routable**) IP address must be globally unique and can be addressed directly by any other computer in the world. A company's web server, or home Internet router for example, would require a public IP address. Within the local network, addresses can be **private** (or **non-routable**) and the web server or router can forward the data going through it to the correct internal device. All devices on the internal network will also have an IP address but this will be private and would not require registration with an **Internet registry**. As such, private IP addresses do not need to be globally unique; they must just be unique within their local network. The common IP blocks for a Class C private network are 192.168.0.0 to 192.168.255.255. Assigning private addresses to internally networked devices conserves the number of unique IPv4 addresses available for Internet-facing devices. A home network printer, for example would be allocated a private IP address to prevent others outside your network from being able to print to it. To allow external access to a privately addressed computer, a **Network Address Translator (NAT)** is required.

> **Q3:** Why would a combined home router/hub device have both a public and a private IP address?

Dynamic Host Configuration Protocol

A **Dynamic Host Configuration Protocol (DHCP)** server is used to automatically assign a **dynamic IP address** from a pool of available addresses to a computer attempting to operate on a public network such as an Internet hotspot. Since IP addresses are in short supply, this system of dynamic addressing enables active computers to request an IP address for the duration they are online and release the address back to the pool for another computer when it is not in use. DHCP also provides the **subnet mask** and other automatic configuration details alongside the IP address, solving problems with manual configuration and centrally handling frequent changes of IP address such as those used with mobile devices moving from one area to another. DHCP is also used on private networks to allocate internal IP addresses to machines (e.g. 192.168.1.x). **Static IP addressing** is uncommon as it permanently allocates a networked computer a scarce IPv4 address.

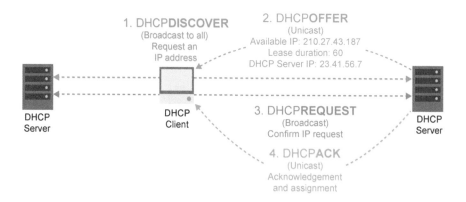

Network Address Translation

Network Address Translation (NAT) is used to convert IP addresses as they pass between a **public address space** (via a router for example) using a public IP address and a LAN with a **private address space**. NAT is required to translate private IP addresses since they are not routable and therefore cannot be used for routing packets on the Internet. Private addresses are also not unique so external servers cannot send packets directly back to a unique private address. An outgoing server request made by a computer on a private network contains its own IP address and port number. The router logs these as an entry in a translation table and swaps the packet IP address and port number for its own external

10-60

IP address and a unique port number. An incoming response, identified by the port number, is then rebadged with the original workstation's internal IP address and port number from the translation table. NAT provides a solution to the lack of public address in IPv4 while we undergo the transition to IPv6 which will afford everyone a unique address. It also offers an additional layer of security by automatically creating a **firewall** between the internal and external networks.

Port forwarding

Port forwarding is commonly a product of **Network Address Translation** when a public computer is trying to communicate with a server operating within a private network. Since there is no direct connection to the server, the NAT needs to forward all incoming requests to a particular IP address and port (for example web requests on port 80) to port 80 of an internal web server using a private IP address. Requests to access the internal server would be sent to the IP address of the external router, which can be programmed to filter out packets destined for certain computers or applications.

Exercises

1. The diagram below shows the physical topology of a Local Area Network connected to the Internet. The LAN uses the IPv4 protocol.

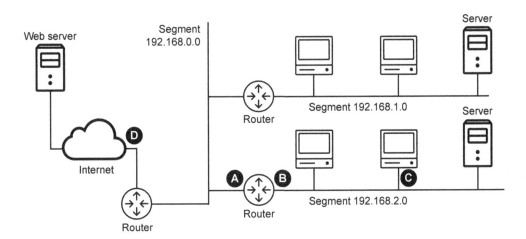

(a) State suitable IP addresses for:

    (i)   The router connection marked A.   [1]

    (ii)   The router connection marked B.   [1]

    (iii)   The Network Interface Card for the terminal marked C.   [1]

    (iv)   The public router connection marked D.   [1]

(b) The combined router and switch device has two IP addresses. One is a public address and the other is a private address.

    Explain the difference between public and private IP addresses.   [2]

(c) The network has been segmented using a technique called 'subnetting'.

    (i)   Explain the advantages to a network administrator of subnetting.   [2]

    (ii)   The first 24 bits of the network's public IP address represent the Network ID. Two further bits are used for the Subnet ID and machines on the network were configured with a subnet mask of 11111111.11111111.11111111.11000000.

    State the number of IP addresses available for the network devices.   [2]

10-60

(d) Computers on the network use the Dynamic Host Configuration Protocol (DHCP) to obtain a public IP address before communicating over the Internet.

    (i)   Give one advantage of using DHCP. [1]

    (ii)   Why are dynamic IP addresses preferred, rather than using static IP addresses? [2]

(e) An FTP server inside a company network contains files that employees can access outside of the office network.

Briefly explain how port forwarding is used to access internal files. [2]

10-60

Chapter 61 – Client server model

Objectives

- Be familiar with the client-server model
- Be familiar with the WebSocket protocol and know why and where it is used
- Understand the principles of Web CRUD applications and Representational State Transfer (REST)
- Compare JSON (JavaScript Object Notation) with XML
- Compare and contrast thin-client computing with thick-client computing

The client-server model

In the client-server model, a client will send a request message to a server which should respond with the data requested or a suitable message otherwise. This is commonly seen when a client browser sends an HTTP request to a web server for web page data or a web resource. The page data is sent back from the HTTP server by way of response and the browser renders the web page on the client's computer. Servers are usually given specific roles based on the data they hold and the service they provide. Common server types include:

- File server
- Email server
- FTP server
- Proxy server
- DHCP server
- Print server
- Database server

10-61

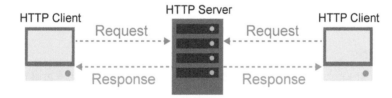

API (Application Programming Interface)

An API is a set of protocols that governs how two applications should interact with one another. An API sets out the format of requests and responses between a client and a server and enables one application to make use of the services of another. An organisation may use the Twitter API to enable relevant tweets to be regularly fed through to a display window within their own website. Price comparison websites may also use an API to gather data from individual company websites in order to display a list of each of them for the consumer.

WebSocket protocol

The WebSocket specification is another example of an API. WebSocket is a modern application layer protocol that facilitates a persistent bi-directional communication channel between the client and the server (usually a web server) over a single line. This is known as full-duplex communication. WebSocket packets are also greatly reduced in size since they use a fraction of the usual header information. All packets communicating via a WebSocket are automatically accepted at either end without the usual need for security checks.

Being able to keep a connection open whilst sending much smaller packets back and forth enables super-fast, real-time and interactive communication commonly used, for example, with online gaming, instant messaging or remote collaborative document editing. The overheads on the HTTP servers running the communication are usually reduced to such a point that fewer web servers are required, therefore saving time in transmission, saving bandwidth and the cost and space of additional unnecessary servers traditionally used with older methods. Reducing data usage is particularly important with mobile data.

Q1: What are the advantages in using the WebSocket protocol with an online auction website?

Web CRUD applications

CRUD is an acronym for Create, Retrieve, Update and Delete. These are the four fundamental operations of a database or content management system. The world has developed a growing desire for online access to database systems using web queries for anything from a shared family calendar on a mobile phone to a full-scale airline seat booking system. Relational databases use four primary SQL (Structured Query Language) statements that can be mapped directly to CRUD.

CRUD	HTTP request methods	SQL database function
(C) Create	POST	INSERT
(R) Retrieve	GET	SELECT
(U) Update	PUT	UPDATE
(D) Delete	DELETE	DELETE

Figure 61.1: Mapping of CRUD operations to HTTP request methods and SQL statements

HTTP request methods

HTTP uses a common standard of verbs or actions such as GET, POST, PUT and DELETE when working with online database servers. Most of the time a browser using the HTTP protocol will perform GET and POST requests only; GET me this web page, GET the images on the page and GET a list of available tickets for the cup final or POST new data to a database. HTTP can also use PUT and DELETE request methods, but less commonly since GET and POST can both be used to perform these functions too.

Q2: Describe how each of the CRUD operations might be used with an online address book application.

Representational State Transfer (REST)

REST is a style of systems design that prescribes the use of HTTP request methods to interact with online databases via a web server. The client computer requires no knowledge of how the server is likely to fulfil the request, how the data is stored or where it will gather the data. This separation allows any client or server to be updated and developed independently of each other without any loss of function. A system or API that conforms to the REST specification can be described as being **RESTful**.

10-61

Connecting a database to a browser with HTTP request methods

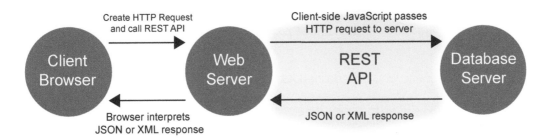

1. A browser makes a client server request from a web server to load a standard web page and all of its resources.

2. The web page HTML file contains some JavaScript which is executed on the client-side.

3. The browser JavaScript calls the RESTful API which enables communication with the server-side database using HTTP requests.

4. The database server responds to the client's HTTP requests with the data in JSON or XML format.

5. The browser renders the JSON or XML data in its own user interface.

Using HTTP methods for RESTful services

Consider the following data stored in a table named `planets` on an online database server:

name	distanceFromSunKM	gravityMS2
Mars	227900000	3.71
Earth	149600000	9.798
Jupiter	778500000	0

An HTTP request treats all of the data as objects and references it in standard URL notation.

HTTP request	Effect
GET http://solarsystem.com/planets/	Return all records in the Planets table
PUT http://solarsystem.com/planets/Jupiter/gravity/24.79	Update the value for Jupiter's gravity to 24.79
DELETE http://solarsystem.com/planets/Jupiter	Remove the record for Jupiter

Q3: What would be the HTTP request to create a new record for Venus? (Tip: Refer to Figure 61.1.)

Comparing JSON (JavaScript Object Notation) with XML (EXtensible Markup Language)

JSON and XML are the two standard methods for transferring data between the server and the web application. Assuming the HTTP requests in the table above had been made upon the data objects on the server, a GET request of GET `http://solarsystem.com/planets/` would now return the values for Mars and Earth. (Jupiter has been deleted.)

10-61

In JSON format, this would look like this:

```
{"planets":[
    {"name": "Mars", "distanceFromSunKM": 227900000, "gravityMS2": 3.71},
    {"name": "Earth", "distanceFromSunKM": 149600000, "gravityMS2": 9.798}
]}
```

In XML format, the response would be defined as:

```
<planets>
    <planet>
      <name>Mars</name>
      <distanceFromSunKM>227900000</distanceFromSunKM>
      <gravityMS2>3.71</gravityMS2>
    </planet>
      <planet>
      <name>Earth</name>
      <distanceFromSunKM>149600000</distanceFromSunKM>
      <gravityMS2>9.798</gravityMS2>
    </planet>
</planets>
```

Q4: Write out the JSON response code for the following GET request:

```
GET http://solarsystem.com/planets/Mars/
```

10-61

Advantages of JSON over XML code format

Whilst XML is still very widely used, having its own advantages over JSON, it is widely agreed that JSON provides a neater solution to data-interchange for the reasons outlined in the table below:

JSON is:	Reason:
Easier for a human to read	JSON code is tidier and easier for a human to read in the data oriented format: `{"object": "value"}`.
More compact	Shorter code with fewer characters. Quicker to transmit. XML fieldnames need to be written out twice.
Easier to create	Simpler syntax and structure. Can also use arrays.
Easier for computers to parse and therefore quicker to parse	Can be parsed by a standard JavaScript function. Numeric values (1) are easier to differentiate from alphanumeric strings ("1").

Despite many advantages of JSON over XML, XML is more flexible that JSON in terms of the structure and the data types that it can be used with.

Thin- versus thick-client computing

The 'thickness' of a client computer refers to the level of processing and storage that it does compared with the server it is connected to. The more processing and storage that a server does, the 'thinner' the client becomes. If all the processing and storage is done by the server, then all that is required for the thinnest-client computer is a very basic machine with very little processor power and no storage. This is often known as a dumb terminal. The decision to go 'thick' or 'thin' rather depends on your specific requirements and each option comes with its own advantages and disadvantages.

Q5: How might you design a mobile GPS navigation app in order to optimise its use, given the advantages and disadvantages of thin- and thick-client systems?

	Advantages	**Disadvantages**
Thin-client	Easy to set up, maintain and add terminals to a network with little installation required locally.	Reliant on the server, so if the server goes down, the terminals lose functionality.
	Software and updates can be installed on the server and automatically distributed to each client terminal.	Requires a very powerful, and reliable server which is expensive.
		Server demand and bandwidth increased.
	More secure since data is all kept centrally in one place.	Maintaining network connections for portable devices consumes more battery power than local data processing.
Thick-client	Robust and reliable, providing greater up-time.	More expensive, higher specification client computers required.
	Can operate without a continuous connection to the server.	Installation of software required on each terminal separately and network administration time is increased.
	Generally better for running more powerful software applications.	Integrity issues with distributed data.

Exercises

1. The following SQL statement returns the Type, Weight and Habitat data for an Aardvark.

    (a) How could this request be written as a URL using CRUD and REST principles? [2]

    ```
    SELECT Type, WeightKG, Food
    FROM Animal
    WHERE Type='Aardvark';
    ```

    (b) Which of the following responses to the request is written in JSON format? [1]

    Response A
    ```
    {"animals":[
       {"type": "Aardvark",
        "weightKG": 50,
        "food": "Termites"}
    ]}
    ```

    Response B
    ```
    <animals>
      <animal>
          <type>Aardvaak</type>
          <weightKG>50</weightKG>
          <food>Termites</food>
      </animal>
    </animals>
    ```

    (c) Give **two** advantages of using JSON over XML for web responses. [2]

2. A travel agency is looking to install a new computer system based on the client-server model for its agents to use for flight and hotel bookings and enquiries at multiple workstations.

    (a) What is meant by the client-server model? [2]

    After some consideration, the company has decided to use a thin-client network.

    (b) Explain how a thin-client network operates. [3]

    (c) How would the decision to use a thin- rather than thick-client network affect the choice of hardware? [2]

3. WebSockets upgrade the HTTP protocol following a handshake between the client cland the server.

    Give **one** feature of the WebSocket protocol and justify an application where it might be used. [3]

Section 11

Databases and software development

In this section:

11

Chapter 62 – Entity relationship modelling

Objectives

- Produce a data model from given data requirements for a simple scenario involving multiple entities
- Produce entity descriptions representing a data model in the form
  Entity1 (Attribute1, Attribute2…)
- Produce entity relationship diagrams representing a data model
- Be able to define the terms attribute, primary key, composite primary key, foreign key

Modelling data requirements

When a systems designer begins work on a new proposed computer system, one of the first things they need to do is to examine the data that needs to be input, processed and stored and determine what the data **entities** are.

Definition: An **entity** is a category of object, person, event or thing of interest to an organisation about which data is to be recorded.

Examples of entities are: Employee, Film, Actor, Product, Recipe, Ingredient.

Each entity in a database system has **attributes**.

Example 1: A dentist's surgery employs several dentists, and an appointments system is required to allow patients to make appointments with a particular dentist.

Entities in this system include **Dentist**, **Patient** and **Appointment**. The attributes of **Dentist** may include Title, Firstname, Surname, Qualification.

Attributes of **Patient** may include Title, Firstname, Surname, Address, Telephone.

Q1: Can you suggest any more attributes for **Patient**?

Q2: What attributes might the entity **Appointment** have?

Entity descriptions

An entity description is normally written using the format

> Entity1 (Attribute1, Attribute2…)

The entity description for **Dentist** is therefore written

> Dentist (Title, Firstname, Surname, Qualification)

Entity identifier and primary key

Each entity needs to have an **entity identifier** which uniquely identifies the entity. In a relational database, the entity identifier is known as the **primary key** and it will be referred to as such in this section. Clearly none of the attributes so far identified for **Dentist** and **Patient** is suitable as a primary key. A numeric or string ID such as D13649 could be used. In the entity description, the primary key is underlined.

> Dentist (DentistID, Title, Firstname, Surname, Qualification)

Q3: Is National Insurance Number a suitable primary key for Patient? If not, why not?

11-62

Relationships between entities

The different entities in a system may be linked in some way, and the two entities are said to be related.

There are only three different 'degrees' of relationship between two entities. A relationship may be

- **One-to-one**   Examples of such a relationship include the relationship between Husband and Wife, Country and Prime Minister.

- **One-to-many**   Examples include the relationship between Mother and Child, Customer and Order, Borrower and Library Book.

- **Many-to-many**   Examples include the relationship between Student and Course, Stock Item and Supplier, Film and Actor.

Entity relationship diagrams

An entity relationship diagram is a diagrammatic way of representing the relationships between the entities in a database. To show the relationship between two entities, both the degree and the name of the relationship need to be specified. E.g. In the first relationship shown below, the degree is one-to-one, the name of the relationship is *in charge of*.

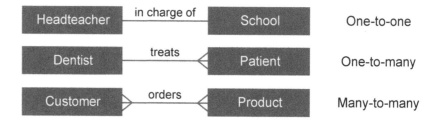

11-62

The concept of a relational database

In a relational database, a separate **table** is created for each entity identified in the system. Where a relationship exists between entities, an extra field called a **foreign key** links the two tables.

Foreign key

A foreign key is an attribute that creates a join between two tables. It is the attribute that is common to both tables, and the primary key in one table is the foreign key in the table to which it is linked.

Example 1

In the one-to-many relationship between Dentist and Patient, the entity on the 'many' side of the relationship will have **DentistID** as an extra attribute. This is the foreign key.

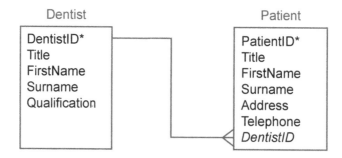

Note that the primary key is indicated by an asterisk, and the foreign key is shown in italics.

Linking tables in a many-to-many relationship

When there is a many-to-many relationship between two entities, tables cannot be directly linked in this way. For example, consider the relationship between **Student** and **Course**. A student takes many courses, and the same course is taken by many students.

Many-to-many

In this case, an extra table is needed to link the **Student** and **Course** tables. We could call this **StudentCourse**, or **Enrolment**, for example.

The three tables will now have attributes something like those shown below:

Student (<u>StudentID</u>, Name, Address)

Enrolment (<u>StudentID</u>, <u>CourseID</u>)

Course (<u>CourseID</u>, Subject, Level)

In this data model, the table linking **Student** and **Course** has two foreign keys, each linking to one of the two main tables. The two foreign keys also act as the primary key of this table. A primary key which consists of more than one attribute is called a **composite primary key**.

Drawing an entity relationship diagram

A database system will frequently involve many different entities linked to each other, and an entity relationship diagram can be drawn to show all the relationships.

11-62

Example 2

A hospital inpatient system may involve entities **Ward**, **Nurse**, **Patient** and **Consultant**. A ward is staffed by many nurses, but each nurse works on only one ward. A patient is in a ward and has many nurses looking after them, as well as a consultant, who sees many patients on different wards.

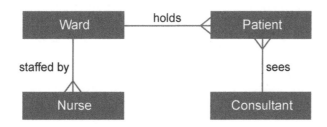

Q4: Is there a relationship between **Patient** and **Nurse**?

Q5: Draw entity-relationship diagrams to illustrate the relationships between

(a) **Product** and **Component**

(b) **Customer**, **Order** and **Product** (An order may be for several different products.)

Exercises

1. An estate agent keeps a database of all the properties it has for sale, the owners of the properties, and all the prospective buyers.

Details about the properties for sale include address, number of bedrooms, type of property, asking price.

Data on prospective buyers include name, telephone, address, type of property required, lower and upper limit for price.

Data on vendors include name, address, telephone.

A fourth entity, **Viewing** holds data about all viewings.

(a) Suggest **three** attributes for the entity **Viewing**.   [3]

(b) Write entity descriptions for each of the entities **Property**, **Vendor**, **Buyer** and **Viewing**. In each case, identify any primary and foreign keys.   [8]

(c) Draw an entity relationship diagram showing relationships between these four entities.   [4]

2. A library plans to set up a database to keep track of its members, books and loans. Entities are defined as follows:

Member (MemberID, Surname, FirstName, Address)

Book (BookID, ISBN, Title, Author)

Loan (MemberID, BookID, loanDate, dueDate)

When the book is returned the loan record is deleted.

(a) Draw an entity relationship diagram showing the relationships between the entities.   [3]

(b) A relational database is created with tables for each of these entities. The key in the Loan table is made up of two fields.

What is the name given to a key that is made up of multiple attributes?   [1]

(c) What is meant by a **foreign** key? Identify a foreign key in one of the tables.   [3]

3. An exam board wants to set up a database to hold data about its courses, exam papers, exam entries, candidates and results. For the purpose of this exercise, assume that each candidate can sit each exam once only. A course may have several exam papers (Comp 1, Comp 2, etc.). You may assume that a candidate enrolled for a course will sit every exam paper associated with that course.

The data to be stored for the candidate are CandidateNumber, FirstName, Surname, DateOfBirth.

The data to be stored for the course are CourseID, Subject, Level

The data held for each individual exam paper includes CourseID, ExamPaperID, DateOfExam, Title, TotalMarks, ExamPaperWeighting.

(a) State an identifier for the entity **ExamPaper**.   [1]

(b) Write an entity description for another entity which will be required to show which courses each student is taking.   [3]

(c) Draw an entity relationship diagram showing the relationships between the entities.   [5]

(d) Write an entity description for a **Results** entity which will store the exam mark that candidates receive for each exam paper.   [2]

Chapter 63 – Relational databases and normalisation

Objectives

- Explain the concept of a relational database

- Normalise relations to third normal form

- Understand why databases are normalised

Relational database design

In a relational database, data is held in tables (also called **relations**) and the tables are linked by means of common attributes.

A **relational database** is a collection of tables in which relationships are modelled by shared attributes.

Conceptually then, one row of a table holds one record. Each column in the table represents one attribute.

e.g. A table holding data about an entity **Book** may have the following rows and columns:

Book

BookID	DeweyCode	Title	Author	DatePublished
88	121.9	Mary Berry Cooks the Perfect	Berry, M	2014
123	345.440	The Paying Guests	Waters, S	2014
300	345.440	Fragile Lies	Elliot, L	2015
657	200.00	Learn French with stories	Bibard, F	2014
777	001.602	GCSE ICT	Barber, A	2010
etc				

To describe the table shown above, you would write

    Book (BookID, DeweyCode, Title, Author, DatePublished)

Note that:

    The **entity name** is shown outside the brackets

    The **attributes** are listed inside the brackets

    The **primary key** is underlined

    The primary key is composed of one or more attributes that will uniquely identify a particular record in the table. (When describing an entity this is called an **entity identifier**.)

In order that a record with a particular primary key can be quickly located in a database, an **index** of primary keys will be automatically maintained by the database software, giving the position of each record according to its primary key.

11-63

Linking database tables

Tables may be linked through the use of a common attribute. This attribute must be a primary key of one of the tables, and is known as a **foreign key** in the second table.

We saw in the last chapter that there are three possible types of relationship between entities: one-to-one, one-to-many and many-to-many.

Normalisation

Normalisation is a process used to come up with the best possible design for a relational database. Tables should be organised in such a way that:

- no data is unnecessarily duplicated (i.e. the same data item held in more than one table)

- data is consistent throughout the database (e.g. a customer is not recorded as having different addresses in different tables of the database). Consistency should be an automatic consequence of not holding any duplicated data. This means that anomalies will not arise when data is inserted, amended or deleted.

- the structure of each table is flexible enough to allow you to enter as many or as few items (for example, components making up a product) as required

- the structure should enable a user to make all kinds of complex queries relating data from different tables

There are three basic stages of normalisation known as first, second and third normal form.

First normal form

A table is in **first normal form (1NF)** if it contains no repeating attribute or groups of attributes.

Example 1

A company manufacturing soft toys buys the component parts (fake fur, glass eyes, stuffing, growl etc.) from different suppliers. Each component may be used in the manufacture of several different toys (teddy bear, dog, duck etc.) Each component comes from a sole supplier.

Sample data to be held in the database is shown in the table:

ProductID	ProductName	CostPrice	Selling Price	CompID	CompName	CompQty	SupplierID	SupplierName
123	Small monkey	2.50	5.95	ST01	Stuffing	30	ABC	ABC Ltd
				G56	Eye (small)	2	BH Glass	Brown & Hill
				FF77	Brown Fur	0.3	FineFur	Fine Toys Ltd
156	Pink kitten	3.10	6.00	ST01	Stuffing	45	ABC	ABC Ltd
				G120	Eye (medium)	2	XYZ Glass	XYZ Ltd
				FF88	Pink Fur	0.35	FineFur	Fine Toys Ltd
				S34	Soundbox	1	Ping Toys	Ping & Co

Table 1

As the first stage in normalization, we need to note that there are repeating groups of attributes in this table; for example, ProductID 123 has three components with IDs ST01, G56 and FF77. We need to split the data into two tables to get rid of the repeating groups.

Note that a table in a relational database may be referred to as a **relation**.

Two entities, **Product** and **Component**, can be identified. These have the following relationship:

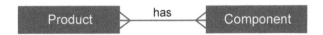

These two entities could be represented in standard notation:

Product (<u>ProductID</u>, ProductName, CostPrice, SellingPrice)

Component (<u>CompID</u>, CompName, SupplierID, SupplierName)

We have not yet put CompQty (the amount or number of each component that is needed to make a particular product) in either table, but we will come to that.

The two tables need to be linked by means of a common attribute, but the problem is that because this is a many-to-many relationship, whichever table we put the link attribute into, there needs to be *more than one* attribute.

e.g.   Product (<u>ProductID</u>, ProductName, CostPrice, SellingPrice, CompQty, ComponentID)

is no good because each toy has several components, so which one would be mentioned?

Similarly, Component (<u>CompID</u>, CompName, SupplierID, SupplierDetails, ProductID)

is no good either because each component is used in a number of different products.

One obvious solution (and unfortunately a bad one) springs to mind. How about allowing space for four components in the record for each product?

Product (<u>ProductID</u>, ProductName, CostPrice, SellingPrice, CompID1, CompQty1, CompID2, CompQty2, CompID3, CompQty3, CompID4, CompQty4)

11-63

> **Q1:** Why is this not a good idea?

This table contains repeating attributes, which are not allowed in first normal form. The attributes ComponentID and CompQty are repeated four times. The table is therefore NOT in first normal form.

It would be represented in standard notation with a line over the repeating attributes:

Product (<u>ProductID</u>, ProductName, CostPrice, SellingPrice, $\overline{\text{CompID, CompQty}}$)

To put the data into first normal form, the repeating attributes must be removed.

Introducing the link table

At this stage it becomes clear why we need a third table to link the two tables **Product** and **Component**.

The three tables now have attributes as follows:

Product (<u>ProductID</u>, ProductName, CostPrice, SellingPrice)

ProductComp (<u>ProductID</u>, <u>CompID</u>, CompQty)

Component (<u>CompID</u>, CompName, SupplierID, SupplierName)

The design is now in 1NF because it contains to repeating attribute or groups of attributes.

> **Q2:** Draw three tables representing these three entities and put the test data from Table 1 in the correct tables.
>
> **Q3:** Which of the primary keys is a composite key?

Dealing with a Many-to-Many relationship

As you get more practice in database design, you will notice that *whenever* two entities have a many-to-many relationship, you will *always* need a link table 'in the middle'. Thus:

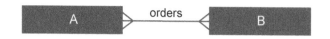

will become:

Second normal form - Partial key dependence test

A table is in **second normal form (2NF)** if it is in first normal form and contains no **partial dependencies**. A partial dependency would mean that one or more of the attributes depends on only part of the primary key, which can only occur if the primary key is a composite key.

The only table in which this could arise is **ProductComp** as this is the only table with a composite primary key. However, the only attribute in this table apart from the primary key is CompQty, which depends both on both parts of the primary key – which product and which particular component in that product.

The tables are therefore now in second normal form.

(To demonstrate tables which are not in second normal form, we'll look at Example 2 shortly.)

11-63

Third normal form - Non-key dependence test

A table is in **third normal form (3NF)** if it is in second normal form and contains no 'non-key dependencies'. A non-key dependency is one where the value of an attribute is determined by the value of another attribute which is not part of the key. 3NF means that:

All attributes are dependent on the key, the whole key, and nothing but the key.

Looking at the **Component** table, the SupplierName attribute is dependent on CompID and not on the SupplierID. It therefore needs to be removed from this relation and a new relation created.

The database, now in third normal form, consists of the following tables:

Product (<u>ProductID</u>, ProductName, CostPrice, SellingPrice)

ProductComp (<u>ProductID</u>, <u>CompID</u>, CompQty)

Component (<u>CompID</u>, CompName, *SupplierID*)

Supplier (<u>SupplierID</u>, SupplierName)

The entity relationship diagram showing the relationships between these four tables in third normal form is shown below. Each entity has its own table.

Example 2

A school plans to keep records of Sports Day events for different years in a database. The data that needs to be held for each event in a particular year is illustrated in the following table:

EventID	Year	EventName	Winner	TimeOrDistance
GA100	2015	Girls Under 14 100m	Claire Gordon	16.1
BJ100	2015	Junior Boys 100m	Marc Harris	13.1

The entity description is:

Event (EventID, Year, EventName, Winner, TimeOrDistance)

The composite primary key is composed of EventID and Year. Winner and TimeOrDistance depend on the whole key.

However, EventName depends only on EventID, not on Year, so this is a partial dependency. This table is therefore not normalised. It does not satisfy the requirement of a table in second normal form, namely that there are no partial dependencies.

Q4: Show how the database may be normalised by writing entity descriptions for each relation. Draw an entity relationship diagram.

The importance of normalisation

A normalised database has major advantages over an un-normalised one.

Maintaining and modifying the database

It is easier to maintain and change a normalised database.

Data integrity is maintained since there is no unnecessary duplication of data. For example, a customer with a particular customer ID will have their personal details stored only once. If the customer changes address, the update needs only to be made to a single table, so there is no possibility of inconsistencies arising with different addresses for the customer being held on different files.

It will also be impossible to insert transactions such as details of an order, for a customer who is not recorded in the database.

Faster sorting and searching

Normalisation will produce smaller tables with fewer fields. This results in faster searching, sorting and indexing operations as there is less data involved.

A further advantage is that holding data only once saves storage space.

Deleting records

A normalised database with correctly defined relationships between tables will not allow records in a table on the 'one' side of a one-to-many relationship to be deleted accidentally. For example, a customer who still has unresolved transactions on file cannot be deleted. This will prevent accidental deletion of a customer who has an unpaid invoice recorded, for example.

Exercises

1. A collector of popular music compact discs (CDs) wishes to store details of the collection in a database in a way that will allow information about the CDs to be extracted.

The data requirements are defined as follows.

- Each compact disc is assigned a catalogue number (unique) and labelled with a title, record company and type of popular music.
- Each compact disc contains one or more tracks.
- A track stores a recording.
- The recording may be a song or some other piece of music.
- A particular track recording features just one named artist.
- The name of each artist to be recorded together with a unique identifier, ArtistID.
- Each song and piece of music may be recorded on different CDs and by different artists.
- A particular CD will never have more than one recording of a particular song or piece of music but may contain tracks featuring the same artist or different artists.
- The title of every song and piece of music in the collection is to be recorded together with the name of the composer of the music and a unique identifier, SongMusicID.
- Each track on a particular CD is assigned a different number with the first always numbered one, the next two and so on.
- The duration of a track recording is recorded.

11-63

A single table, CDTable, was constructed initially in a relational database. The figure below shows the structure of this table and a few entries.

Catalogue No	Title	Record Company	Music Type	Track No	Track Duration	SongMusic ID	SongMusic Title	Composer Name	ArtistID	Artist Name
1	Quiet Time	ABC	Grunge	1	120	5	Action Man	Smith	1	Eric Ant
				2	150	8	Dedicated Woman	Williams	1	Eric Ant
								Brown	2	Rick Bana
				3	300	23	Last waltz		2	Rick Bana
				4	360	45	Shout	Nichols	2	Rick Bana
2	Running Scared	ABC	Rock	1	150	8	Dedicated Woman	Williams	2	Rick Bana
				2	140	4	Glad Tidings	Fox	2	Rick Bana
				3	280	12	Zulu	Vermouth	3	Rick Bana
				...	300	...	...	...	...	...
3	Sunshine Blues	BCD	Grunge	1	120	26	Jaded	Orchard	5	Yana Smit
				...	...	...	...	...	...	...
...	...	...	...	1	...	120	...	...	...	...
				...	...	...	...	...	...	...
...	...	...	...	1	...	45	Shout	...	...	...
				...	...	...	...	...	...	...
...	...	...	...	1	...	3	...	...	...	...
				...	...	...	...	...	...	...

(a) Which of the column headings in CDTable would be suitable as a primary key? [2]

(b) CDTable is not in first normal form. Explain. [2]

After normalisation the database contains the four tables based on the entities:

CompactDisc, CD-Track, SongMusic, Artist

(c) Using a copy of the partially complete entity relationship diagram below as an aid, show the degree of **four** more relationships which exist between the given entities.

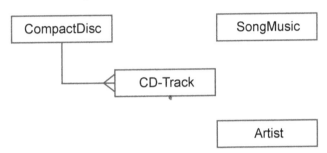

(d) Using the following format

TableName(PrimaryKey, Non-key Attribute 1, Non-key Attribute 2, etc)

Describe tables, stating all attributes, for the following entities underlining the primary key in each case.

(i)	CompactDisc	[2]
(ii)	SongMusic	[2]
(iii)	Artist	[2]
(iv)	CD-Track	[4]

(e) Using the SQL commands **SELECT**, **FROM**, **WHERE**, write an SQL statement to query the database tables for the track numbers, SongMusicIDs and ArtistIDs for a given CD catalogue number, 15438.[3]

(Leave part (e) until you have completed the next chapter.)

AQA Computing Paper 3 Qu 13 Summer 2001

2. A college department wishes to create a database to hold information about students and the courses they take. The relationship between students and courses is shown in the following entity relationship diagram.

Each course has a tutor who is in charge of the course.

Sample data held on the database is shown in the table below.

Student Number	Student Name	DateOfBirth	Gender	Course Number	CourseName	TeacherID	Teacher Name
1111	Bell, K	14-01-1998	M	COMP23	Java1	8563	Davey,A
2222	Cope, F	12-08-1997	F	COMP23	Java1	8563	Davey,A
				COMP16	Intro to OOP	2299	Ross,M
				G101	Animation	1567	Day,S
3333	Behr,K	31-07-1996	M	Comp16	Intro to OOP	2299	Ross,M
				Comp34	Database Design	3370	Blaine, N

(a) Show how the data may be rearranged into relations which are in third normal form. [6]

(b) State **two** properties that the tables in a fully normalised database must have. [2]

11-63

Chapter 64 – Introduction to SQL

Objectives

- Be able to use SQL to retrieve data from multiple tables of a relational database

SQL

SQL, or **Structured Query Language** (pronounced either as S-Q-L or Sequel) is a **declarative language** used for querying and updating tables in a relational database. It can also be used to create tables. In this chapter, we will look at SQL statements used in querying a database.

The tables shown in Tables 1, 2 and 3 below will be used to demonstrate some SQL statements. The tables are part of a database used by a retailer to store details of CDs in a database that will allow information about the CDs to be extracted. This is a simplified version of the database described in Exercise 1 in the previous chapter.

The four entities **CD**, **CDSong**, **Song** and **Artist** are connected by the following relationships:

Figure 1

The **CD** table is shown below.

CDNumber	CDTitle	RecordCompany	DatePublished
CD14356	Shadows	ABC	06/05/2014
CD19998	Night Turned Day	GHK	24/03/2015
CD25364	Autumn	ABC	11/10/2015
CD34512	Basic Poetry	GHK	01/02/2016
CD56666	The Lucky Ones	DEF	16/02/2016
CD77233	Lucky Me	ABC	24/05/2015
CD77665	Flying High	DEF	31/07/2015

*Table 1: **CD** table*

SELECT .. FROM .. WHERE

The SELECT statement is used to extract a collection of fields from a given table. The basic syntax of this statement is

SELECT	*list of fields to be displayed*
FROM	*list the table or tables the data will come from*
WHERE	*list of search criteria*
ORDER BY	*list the fields that the results are to be sorted on (default is Ascending order)*

11-64

Example 1

```
SELECT CDTitle, RecordCompany, DatePublished
FROM CD
WHERE DatePublished BETWEEN #01/01/2015# AND #31/12/2015#
ORDER BY CDTitle
```

This will return the following records:

CDTitle	RecordCompany	DatePublished
Autumn	ABC	11/10/2015
Flying High	DEF	31/07/2015
Lucky Me	ABC	24/05/2015
Night Turned Day	GHK	24/03/2015

Conditions

Conditions in SQL are constructed from the following operators:

Symbol	Meaning	Example	Notes
=	Equal to	CDTitle = "Autumn"	Different implementations use single or double quotes
>	Greater than	DatePublished > #01/01/2015#	The date is enclosed in quote marks or, in Access, # symbols.
<	Less than	DatePublished < #01/01/2015#	
<>	Not equal to	RecordCompany <> "ABC"	
>=	Greater than or equal to	DatePublished >= #01/01/2015#	
<=	Less than or equal to	DatePublished <= #01/01/2015#	
IN	Equal to a value within a set of values	RecordCompany IN ("ABC", "DEF")	
LIKE	Similar to	CDTitle LIKE "S*"	Finds Shadows (wildcard operator varies and can be %)
BETWEEN…AND	Within a range, including the two values which define the limits	DatePublished BETWEEN #01/01/2015# AND #31/12/2015#	
IS NULL	Field does not contain a value	RecordCompany IS NULL	
AND	Both expressions must be true for the entire expression to be judged true	DatePublished > #01/01/2015# AND RecordCompany = "ABC"	
OR	If either or both of the expressions are true, the entire expression is judged true.	RecordCompany = "ABC" OR RecordCompany = "DEF"	Equivalent to RecordCompany IN ("ABC", "DEF")
NOT	Inverts truth	RecordCompany NOT IN ("ABC", "DEF")	

Q1: SQL statements are written in the format

```
SELECT *
FROM table
WHERE condition
```

Write a query which will display all fields of records in the CD table published by the ABC or GHK record company in 2014-2015. (Note that the * means 'Display all fields in the record'.) Referring the data in *Table 1*, what are the CDNumbers of the records returned by this query?

Specifying a sort order

ORDER BY gives you control over the order in which records appear in the Answer table. If for example you want the records to be displayed in ascending order of CDTitle and within that, descending order of DatePublished, you would write, for example:

```
SELECT *
FROM CD
WHERE DatePublished < #31/12/2015#
ORDER BY RecordCompany, DatePublished Desc;
```

This would produce the following results:

CDNumber	CDTitle	RecordCompany	DatePublished
CD25364	Autumn	ABC	11/10/2015
CD77233	Lucky Me	ABC	24/05/2014
CD14356	Shadows	ABC	06/05/2014
CD77665	Flying High	DEF	31/07/2015
CD19998	Night Turned Day	GHK	24/03/2015

Extracting data from several tables

So far we have only taken data from one table. The **Song** and **Artist** tables in the database have the following contents:

SongID	SongTitle	ArtistID	MusicType
S1234	Waterfall	A318	Americana
S1256	Shake it	A123	Heavy Metal
S1258	Come Away	A154	Americana
S1344	Volcano	A134	Art Pop
S1389	Complicated Game	A318	Americana
S1392	Ghost Town	A123	Heavy Metal
S1399	Gentle Waves	A134	Art Pop
S1415	Right Here	A134	Art Pop
S1423	Clouds	A315	Art Pop
S1444	Sheet Steel	A334	Heavy Metal
S1456	Here with you	A154	Art Pop

Table 2: **Song** table

ArtistID	ArtistName
A123	Fred Bates
A134	Maria Okello
A154	Bobby Harris
A315	Jo Morris
A318	JJ
A334	Rapport

Table 3: **Artist** table

Using SQL you can combine data from two or more tables, by specifying which table the data is held in. For example, suppose you wanted SongTitle, ArtistName and MusicType for all *Art Pop* music. When more than one table is involved, SQL uses the syntax tablename.fieldname. (The table name is optional unless the field name appears in more than one table.)

11-64

```
SELECT Song.SongTitle, Artist.ArtistName, Song.MusicType
FROM Song, Artist
WHERE (Song.ArtistID = Artist.ArtistID) AND (Song.MusicType = "Art Pop");
```

The condition `Song.ArtistID = Artist.ArtistID` provides the link between the Song and Artist tables so that the artist's name corresponding to the ArtistID in the **Song** table can be found in the Artist table. This will produce the following results:

SongTitle	ArtistName	MusicType
Volcano	Maria Okello	Art Pop
Gentle Waves	Maria Okello	Art Pop
Right Here	Maria Okello	Art Pop
Clouds	Jo Morris	Art Pop
Here with you	Bobby Harris	Art Pop

Q2: Write an SQL query which will give the SongTitle, ArtistName, MusicType of all songs by *JJ* or *Rapport*, sorted by ArtistName and SongTitle.

The fourth table in the database is the table **CDSong** which links the songs to one or more of the CDs.

CDNumber	SongID
CD14356	S1234
CD14356	S1258
CD14356	S1415
CD19998	S1234
CD19998	S1389
CD19998	S1423
CD19998	S1456
CD25364	S1256
CD25364	S1392
CD34512	S1392
CD34512	S1234
CD34512	S1389
CD34512	S1444
CD77233	S1256
CD77233	S1344
CD77233	S1399
CD77233	S1456

*Table 4: **CDSong** table*

Example 2

We can make a search to find the CDNumbers and titles of all the CDs containing the song *Waterfall*, sung by JJ.

```
SELECT Song.SongID, Song.SongTitle, Artist.ArtistName, CDSong.CDNumber,
CD.CDTitle
FROM Song, Artist, CDSong, CD
WHERE CDSong.CDNumber = CD.CDNumber
   AND CDSong.SongID = Song.SongID
   AND Artist.ArtistID = Song.ArtistID
   AND Song.SongTitle = "Waterfall";
```

11-64

This will produce the following results:

SongID	SongTitle	ArtistName	CDNumber	CDTitle
S1234	Waterfall	JJ	CD14356	Shadows
S1234	Waterfall	JJ	CD19998	Night Turned Day
S1234	Waterfall	JJ	CD34512	Basic Poetry

Note that in the **SELECT** statement, it does not matter whether you specify `Song.SongID` or `CDSong.SongID` since they are connected. The same is true of `CDSong.CDNumber` and `CD.CDNumber`. The three Boolean conditions `CDSong.CDNumber = CD.CDNumber`, `CDSong.SongID = Song.SongID` and `Artist.ArtistID = Song.ArtistID` are required to specify the relationships between the data tables. See the Entity Relationship Diagram in Figure 1 above.

Exercises

1. Customers placing orders with ABC Ltd for ABC's products have their orders recorded by ABC in a database.

The data requirements for the database system are defined as follows:

- Each product is assigned a unique product code, ProductId and has a product description.
- The quantity in stock of a particular product is recorded.
- Each customer is assigned a unique customer code, CustomerId and has their name, address and telephone number recorded.
- An order placed by a customer will be for one or more products.
- ABC Ltd assigns a unique code to each customer order, ABCOrderNo.
- A customer placing an order must supply a code, CustomerOrderNo, which the customer uses to identify the particular order.
- A customer may place one or more orders.
- Each new order from a particular customer will have a different customer order code but two different customers may use, independently, the same values of customer order code.
- Whether an order has been despatched or not will be recorded.
- A particular order will contain one or more lines.
- Each line is numbered, the first is one, the second is two, and so on.
- Each line will reference a specific product and specify the quantity ordered.
- A specific product reference will appear only once in any particular order placed with ABC Ltd.

After normalisation the database contains four tables based on the entities:

Customer, Product, Order, OrderLine

(a) The figure below is a partially complete entity relationship diagram. Show the degree of **three** more relationships which exist between the given entities.

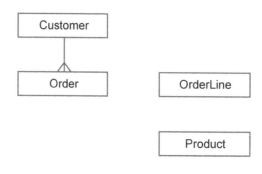

[3]

11-64

(b) Using the following format:

TableName (Primary Key, Non-key Attribute1, Non-key Attribute2, etc)

describe tables, stating all attributes, for the following entities underlining the primary key in each case.

(i) Product [2]

(ii) Customer [2]

(iii) Order [3]

(iv) OrderLine [4]

(c) Using the SQL commands SELECT, FROM, WHERE, ORDER BY, write an SQL statement to query the database tables for all customer names where the orders have been despatched.

The result of the query is to be ordered in ascending order of ABCOrderNo. [6]

AQA CPT5 Qu 8 June 2002

2. A school keeps records of school trips on a database. There are four tables on the database named PUPIL, TRIP, TEACHER, PUPILTRIP, defined as follows:

PUPIL (PupilID, PupilSurname, PupilFirstName)

TRIP (TripID, Description, StartDate, EndDate, Destination, NumberOfStudents, TeacherID)

TEACHER (TeacherID, Title, FirstName, Surname)

PUPILTRIP (PupilID, TripID)

(a) Draw an entity relationship diagram showing the relationship between the entities.

(b) Write SQL statements for each of the following operations:

(i) find the first name and surname of all pupils who went on a trip with TripID 14. [4]

(ii) find all the trips for which the teacher with surname "Black" has been in charge, giving teacher's title and surname, trip description and start date, sorted in descending order of start date. [4]

(iii) find the firstnames and surnames of all the pupils who went on any trip with "Year 7" in the description (e.g. "Year 7 Geography field trip" in May 2015, showing the firstname and surname of the teacher in charge. [6]

11-64

Chapter 65 – Defining and updating tables using SQL

Objectives

- Be able to use SQL to define a database table
- Be able to use SQL to update, insert and delete data from multiple tables of a relational database
- Know that a client server database system provides simultaneous access to the database for multiple clients
- Know how concurrent access can be controlled to preserve the integrity of the database

Defining a database table

The following example shows how to create a new database table.

Example 1

Use SQL to create a table named **Employee**, which has four columns: EmpID (a compulsory *int* field which is the primary key), Name (a compulsory *character* field of length 20), HireDate (an optional *date* field) and Salary (an optional *real number* field).

```
CREATE TABLE Employee
(
EmpID      INTEGER NOT NULL, PRIMARY KEY,
EmpName    VARCHAR(20) NOT NULL,
HireDate   DATE,
Salary     CURRENCY
)
```

Data types

Some of the most commonly used data types are described in the table below. (The data types vary depending on the specific implementation.)

Data type	Description	Example
CHAR(n)	Character string of fixed length n	ProductCode CHAR(6)
VARCHAR(n)	Character string variable length, max. n	Surname VARCHAR(25)
BOOLEAN	TRUE or FALSE	ReviewComplete BOOLEAN
INTEGER, INT	Integer	Quantity INTEGER
FLOAT	Number with a floating decimal point	Length FLOAT (10,2) (maximum number of digits is 10 and maximum number after decimal point is 2)
DATE	Stores Day, Month, Year values	HireDate DATE
TIME	Stores Hour, Minute, Second values	RaceTime TIME
CURRENCY	Formats numbers in the currency used in your region	EntryFee CURRENCY

11-65

Altering a table structure

The ALTER TABLE statement is used to add, delete or modify columns (i.e. fields) in an existing table.

To add a column (field):

```
ALTER TABLE Employee
ADD Department VARCHAR(10)
```

To delete a column:

```
ALTER TABLE Employee
DROP COLUMN HireDate
```

To change the data type of a column:

```
ALTER TABLE Employee
MODIFY COLUMN EmpName VARCHAR(30) NOT NULL
```

> **Q1:** Use SQL to create a table called **Student** which is defined as follows:
>
> | | | |
> |---|---|---|
> | StudentID | 6 characters | (Primary key) |
> | Surname | 20 characters | |
> | FirstName | 15 characters | |
> | DateOfBirth | Date | |
>
> **Q2:** Write an SQL statement to add a new column named YearGroup, of type Integer.

Defining linked tables

If you set up several tables, you can link tables by creating foreign keys.

Example 2

Suppose that an extra table is to be added to the Employee database which lists the training courses offered by the company. A third table shows which date an employee attended a particular course.

The structure of the **Employee** table is:

EmpID	Integer (Primary key)
Name	30 characters maximum
HireDate	Date
Salary	Currency
Department	30 characters maximum

The structure of the **Course** table is:

CourseID	6 characters, fixed length (Primary key)
CourseTitle	30 characters maximum (must be entered)
OnSite	Boolean

The structure of the **CourseAttendance** table is:

CourseID	6 characters, fixed length (foreign key)
EmpID	Integer (foreign key) Course ID and EmpID form a composite primary key
CourseDate	Date (note that the same course may be run several times on different dates)

The **CourseAttendance** table is created using the SQL statements:

```
CREATE TABLE CourseAttendance
(
CourseID      CHAR(6) NOT NULL,
EmpID         INTEGER NOT NULL,
CourseDate    DATE,
FOREIGN KEY CourseID REFERENCES Course(CourseID),
FOREIGN KEY EmpID REFERENCES Employee(EmpID),
PRIMARY KEY (CourseID, EmpID)
)
```

Q3: Write the SQL statements to create the Course table.

Inserting, updating, and deleting data using SQL

The SQL INSERT INTO statement

This statement is used to insert a new record in a database table. The syntax is:

INSERT INTO *tableName (column1, column2, ...)*
VALUES *(value1, value2, ...)*

Example: add a record for employee number 1122, Bloggs, who was hired on 1/1/2001 for the technical department at a salary of £18000.

```
INSERT INTO Employee (EmpID, Name, HireDate, Salary, Department)
VALUES (1122, "Bloggs", #1/1/2001#, 18000, "Technical")
```

Note that if all the fields are being added in the correct order you would not need the field names in the brackets above to be specified. INSERT INTO Employee would be sufficient

Example: add a record for employee number 1125, Cully, who was hired on 1/1/2001. Salary and Department are not known.

```
INSERT INTO Employee (EmpID, Name, HireDate)
VALUES (1125, "Cully", #1/1/2001#)
```

The SQL Update statement

This statement is used to update a record in a database table. The syntax is:

UPDATE *tableName*
SET *column1 = value1, column2 = value2, ...*
WHERE *columnX = value*

Example: increase all salaries of members of the Technical department by 10%

```
UPDATE Employee
SET Salary = Salary*1.1
WHERE Department = "Technical"
```

Example: Update the record for the employee with ID 1122, who has moved to Administration.

```
UPDATE Employee
SET Department = "Administration"
WHERE EmpID = 1122
```

11-65

The SQL Delete statement

This statement is used to delete a record from a database table. The syntax is:

```
DELETE FROM tableName
WHERE  columnX = value
```

Example: Delete the record for Bloggs, Employee ID 1122.

```
DELETE FROM Employee
WHERE EmpID = 1122
```

Q4: The table Student is defined below:

StudentID	6 characters	(Primary key)
Surname	20 characters	
FirstName	15 characters	
DateOfBirth	Date	

(a) Use SQL to add a record for Jennifer Daley, StudentID AB1234, Date of Birth 23/06/2005.

(b) Update this record, the student's name is Jane, not Jennifer.

(c) Add a new column DateStarted to the table, of type DATE.

Client-Server databases

Many modern database management systems provide an option for client-server operation. Using a client-server Database Management System (DBMS), DBMS server software runs on the network server, and DBMS client software runs on individual workstations. The server software processes requests for data searches and reports that originate from individual workstations running DBMS client software. For example, a car dealer might want to search the manufacturer's database to find out whether there are any cars of a particular specification available. The DBMS client refers this request to the DBMS server, which searches for the information and sends it back to the client workstation. Once the information is at the workstation, the dealer can sort the list and produce a customised report. If the DBMS did not have client-server capability, the entire database would be copied to the workstation and software held on the workstation would search for the requested data – involving a large amount of time being spent on transmitting irrelevant data and probably a longer search using a less powerful machine.

The advantages of a client-server database are, therefore:

- the consistency of the database is maintained because only one copy of the data is held (on the server) rather than a copy at each workstation

- an expensive resource (powerful computer and large database) can be made available to a large number of users

- Access rights and security can be managed and controlled centrally

- Backup and recovery can be managed centrally

Potential problems with client-server databases

Allowing multiple users to simultaneously update a database table may cause one of the updates to be lost unless measures are taken to prevent this.

When an item is updated, the entire record (indeed the whole **block** in which the record is physically held) will be copied into the user's own local memory area at the workstation. When the record is saved, the block is rewritten to the file server. Imagine the following situation:

11-65

User A accesses a customer record, thereby causing it to be copied into the memory at his/her workstation, and starts to type in a new address for the customer.

User B accesses the same customer record, and alters the credit limit and then saves the record and calls up the next record that needs updating.

User A completes the address change, and saves the record.

> **Q5:** What state will the record be in? (i.e. which address and credit limit will it hold?)

There are several methods which may be employed to avoid updates being lost.

Record locks

Record locking is the technique of preventing simultaneous access to objects in a database in order to prevent updates being lost or inconsistencies in the data arising. In its simplest form, a record is locked whenever a user retrieves it for editing or updating. Anyone else attempting to retrieve the same record is denied access until the transaction is completed or cancelled.

Problems with record locking

If two users are attempting to update two records, a situation can arise in which neither can proceed, known as **deadlock**. Suppose a bank clerk is updating Customer A's record with a transfer to Customer B's account. Meanwhile a second bank clerk is trying to update Customer B's record, as he needs to transfer money to Customer A's account.

User1	User2
locks Customer A's record	locks Customer B's record
tries to access Customer B's record	tries to access Customer A's record
waits ..	waits ..

DEADLOCK!

The DBMS must recognise when this situation has occurred and take action. **Serialisation**, **timestamp ordering** or **commitment ordering** may be used.

Serialisation

This is a technique which ensures that transactions do not overlap in time and therefore cannot interfere with each other or lead to updates being lost. A transaction cannot start until the previous one has finished. It can be implemented using **timestamp ordering**.

Timestamp ordering

Whenever a transaction starts, it is given a timestamp, so that if two transactions affect the same object (for example record or table), the transaction with the earlier timestamp should be applied first.

In order to ensure that transactions are not lost, every object in the database has a **read timestamp** and a **write timestamp**, which are updated whenever an object in a database is read or written.

When a transaction starts, it reads the data from a record causing the read timestamp to be set. Before it writes the updated data back to the record it will check the read timestamp. If this is not the same as the value that was saved when this transaction started, it will know that another transaction is also taking place on the record. A range of potential problems can thus be identified and avoided.

Commitment ordering

This is another serialisation technique used to ensure that transactions are not lost when two or more users are simultaneously trying to access the same database object. Transactions are ordered in terms of their dependencies on each other as well as the time they were initiated. It can be used to prevent deadlock by blocking one request until another is completed.

Exercises

1. A company sells furniture to customers of its store. The store does not keep furniture in stock. Instead, a customer places an order at the store and the company then orders the furniture required from its suppliers. When the ordered furniture arrives at the store a member of staff telephones or emails the customer to inform them that it is ready for collection. Customers often order more than one type of furniture on the same order, for example a sofa and two chairs.

Details of the furniture, customers and orders are to be stored in a relational database using the following four relations:

Furniture (<u>FurnitureID</u>, FurnitureName, Category, Price, SupplierName)

CustomerOrder (<u>OrderID</u>, CustomerID, Date)

CustomerOrderLine (<u>OrderID</u>, <u>FurnitureID</u>, Quantity)

Customer (<u>CustomerID</u>, CustomerName, EmailAddress, TelephoneNumber)

(a) These relations are in Third Normal Form (3NF).

    (i) What does this mean? [2]

    (ii) Why is it important that the relations in a relational database are in Third Normal Form? [2]

(b) On the incomplete Entity Relationship diagram below show the degree of any **three** relationships that exist between the entities. [3]

| Furniture | | CustomerOrder |

| Customer | | CustomerOrderLine |

(c) Complete the following Data Definition Language (DDL) statement to create the Furniture relation, including the key field.

```
CREATE TABLE Furniture (
```
[3]

(d) A fault has been identified with the product that has FurnitureID number 10765. The manager needs a list of the names and telephone numbers of all the customers who have purchased this item of furniture so that they can be contacted. This list should contain no additional details and must be presented in alphabetical order of the names of the customers.

Write an SQL query that will produce this list. [6]

AQA Unit 3 Qu 9 June 2013

2. (a) Explain how, in a client-server database with multiple users, an update made by one user may not be recorded if the DBMS does not have measures in place to ensure the integrity of the database. [3]

(b) Explain what is meant by deadlock and how this can arise. [2]

(c) Name and describe briefly a method of preventing this from happening. [2]

11-65

Chapter 66 – Systematic approach to problem solving

Objectives

- Describe aspects of software development
- Explain the prototyping/agile approach that may be used in the analysis, design and implementation of a system
- Understand what is meant by data modelling
- Know the criteria for evaluating a computer system

Aspects of software development

There is an infinite variety of different types of problem that can be solved using a computer. Whether you are developing a website for a new company selling goods or services, designing a simulation of a physics experiment, building a control system using a microprocessor or something else, all software projects have certain aspects in common.

Analysis

Before a problem can be solved, it must be defined. The requirements of the system that solves the problem must be established. In the case of a data processing system, or for example the construction of a website, this could cover:

- the **data** – its origin, uses, volumes and characteristics
- the **procedures** – what is done, where, when and how, and how errors and exceptions are handled
- **the future** – development plans and expected growth rates
- **problems** with any existing system

In the case of a different type of problem such as a simulation or game, the requirements will still need to cover a similar set of considerations.

Agile modelling

At all the stages of analysis, design and implementation, an **agile approach** may be adopted, as the stages of software development may not be completed in a linear sequence. It might be that some analysis is done and then some parts of a system are designed and implemented while other parts are still being analysed and then, for example, implementation and testing may be intermixed. The developer may then go back to design another aspect of the system.

Throughout the process, feedback will be obtained from the user; this is an **iterative process** during which changes made are incremental as the next part of the system is built. Typically the software developers do just enough modelling at the start of the project to make sure that the system is clearly understood by both themselves and the users.

11-66

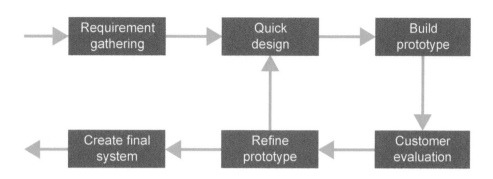

At each stage, a **prototype** is built with user participation to ensure that the system is being developed in line with what the user wants. The success of the software development depends on

- **keeping the model simple**, and not trying to incorporate features which may come in useful at a later date

- **rapid feedback from the user**

- understanding that user requirements may change during development as they are forced to consider their needs in detail

- being prepared to make **incremental changes** as the model develops

Design

Depending on the type of project, the systems designer may consider some or all of the following:

- **processing:** the algorithms and appropriate modular structure for the solution, specifying modules with clear documented interfaces

- **data structures:** how data will be held and how it will be accessed – for example in a dynamic data structure such as a queue or tree, or in a file or database

- **output:** content, format, sequence, frequency, medium (e.g. screen or hard copy) etc.

- **input:** volume, frequency, documents used, input methods;

- **user interface:** screens and dialogues, menus, special-purpose requirements

- **security:** how the data is to be kept secure from accidental corruption or deliberate tampering or hacking

- **hardware:** selection of an appropriate configuration

Modelling data requirements

What exactly is "an abstract representation of a problem"? We cannot easily represent the world as it "really is", but we can make abstractions and simplifications so that we can structure and manipulate relevant data to help us achieve a particular goal.

> **Q1:** How could you model the relationships between several generations of a family so that they can be clearly understood?

Whatever the proposed data structures are, modelling will involve deciding what data needs to be held and how the data items are related to each other.

In addition to modelling data requirements, a **prototype of the user interface** may be built so that the user can get a clear idea of how they will interact with the system, how data will be input and how arduous this task might be under the proposed system. Once again user involvement is crucial, and at this stage changes to the prototype should be straightforward.

Implementation

Once the design has been agreed, the programs can be coded. A clear focus needs to be maintained on the ultimate goal of the project, without users or programmers being sidetracked into creating extra features which might be useful, or possible future requirements. "*Solve the critical path first!*"

Programmers will need to be flexible in accepting user feedback and making changes to their programs as problems or design flaws are detected. In even a moderately complex system it is hard to envision how everything will work together, so iterative changes at every stage are a normal part of a prototyping/ agile approach.

Testing

Testing is carried out at each stage of the development process. Testing the implementation is covered in Chapter 10. Once all the programs have been tested with normal, boundary and erroneous data, unit testing, module testing and system testing will also be carried out.

The system then needs to be tested by the user to ensure that it meets the specification.

This is known as **acceptance testing**. It involves testing with data supplied by the end user rather than data designed especially for testing purposes.

It has the following objectives:

- to confirm that the system delivered meets the original customer specifications
- to find out whether any major changes in operating procedures will be needed
- to test the system in the environment in which it will run, with realistic volumes of data

Testing is an iterative process, with each stage in the test process being repeated when modifications have to be made owing to errors coming to light at a subsequent stage.

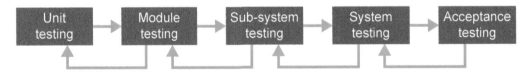

Evaluation

The evaluation may include a post-implementation review, which is a critical examination of the system three to six months after it has been put into operation. This waiting period allows users and technical staff to learn how to use the system, get used to new ways of working and understand the new procedures required. It allows management a chance to evaluate the usefulness of the reports and on-line queries that they can make, and go through several 'month-end' periods when various routine reports will be produced. Shortcomings of the system, if there are any, will be becoming apparent at all levels of the organisation, and users will want a chance to air their views and discuss improvements. The solution should be evaluated on the basis of **effectiveness**, **usability** and **maintainability**.

11-66

The post-implementation review will focus on the following:

- a comparison of the system's actual performance with the anticipated performance objectives
- an assessment of each aspect of the system against preset criteria
- errors which were made during system development
- unexpected benefits and problems

Exercises

1. (a) Explain what is meant by the **prototyping/agile approach** to system analysis and design.   [4]

(b) What are the advantages of this approach?   [4]

2. A systems analyst/developer is planning a system for the administration of student courses to be used in an office in a college.

(a) Other than data modelling, describe **three** tasks that may be carried out by the analyst to establish the requirements of the system.   [6]

(b) A database will be used in the implementation of the system. Describe the steps involved in creating a data model.   [3]

11-66

Section 12

OOP and functional programming

In this section:

12

Chapter 67 – Basic concepts of object-oriented programming

Objectives

- Be familiar with the basic concepts of object-oriented programming, such as class, object, instantiation and encapsulation

Procedural programming

Programming languages have been evolving ever since the development of assembly languages. High level languages such as Basic and Pascal are known as **procedural languages**, and a program written in one of these languages is written using a series of step-by-step instructions on how to solve the problem. This is usually broken down into a number of smaller modules, and the program then consists of a series of calls to procedures or functions, each of which may in turn call other procedures or functions.

In this method of programming, the data is held in separate primitive variables such as integer or char, or in data structures such as array or list. The data may be accessible by all procedures in the program (**global** variables) or **local** to a particular subroutine. Changes made to global data may affect other parts of the program, either intentionally or unintentionally, and may mean other subroutines have to be modified.

Object-oriented programming

In object-oriented programming, the world is viewed as a collection of **objects**. An object might be a person, animal, place, concept or event, for example. It could be something more abstract like a bank account or a data structure such as a stack or queue that the programmer wishes to implement.

An object-oriented program is composed of a number of interacting objects, each of which is responsible for its own data and the operations on that data. Program code in an object-oriented program creates the objects and allows the objects to communicate with each other by sending messages and receiving answers. All the processing that is carried out in the program is done by objects.

Object attributes and behaviours

Each object will have its own **attributes**. The attributes of a car might include its make, engine size, colour, etc. The attributes of a person could include first name, last name, date of birth.

An object has a **state**. A radio, for example, may be on or off, tuned to a particular station, set to a certain volume. A bank account may have a particular balance, say £54.20 and a credit limit of £300.

Q1: What attributes might be assigned to the following objects?

(a) Cat

(b) Rectangle

(c) Hotel booking

An object has **behaviours**. These are the actions that can be performed by an object; for example, a cat can walk, pounce, catch mice, purr, miaow and so on.

12-67

Classes

A **class** is a blueprint or template for an object, and it defines the **attributes** and **behaviours** (known as **methods**) of objects in that class. An attribute is data that is associated with the class, and a method is a functionality of the class – something that it can do, or that can be done with it.

For example, a stock control system might be used by a bookshop for recording the items that it receives into stock from suppliers and sells to customers. The only information that the stock class will hold in this simplified system is the stock ID number, stock category (books, stationery, etc.), description, and quantity in stock.

Part of a sample definition of a class named `StockItem` is defined below. Program coding will vary according to the language used.

```
* Stock class used to model a simple stock control system,
* allowing stock to be added and sold.

StockItem = Class
* A function may take one or more parameters. It returns a value
* A procedure may take one or more parameters. It does not return a value
        Public
            Function GetQtyInStock
            Procedure StockItem(String aStockID,
                String aCategory, String aDescription, Integer aQty)
            Procedure ReceiveStock (Integer aQty)
            Procedure SellStock (Integer aQty)
* instance variables (properties/attributes)
        Private
            StockID:String
            Category: String
            Description: String
            QtyInStock: Integer
    End
```

In this part of the class definition, each of the attributes is given a variable type – here the first three attributes are of type `String` and `QtyInStock` is `Integer`.

As a general rule, instance variables or attributes are declared **private** and most methods **public**, so that other classes may use methods belonging to another class but may not see or change their attributes. This principle of **information hiding**, where other classes cannot directly access the attributes of another class when they are declared private, is an important feature of object-oriented programming.

A **constructor** is used to create objects in a class. In the above example the constructor is called `StockItem`; in many programming languages the constructor must have the same name as the class. In the pseudocode used here, methods are defined as either procedures, which are "setter" methods, or functions, which are "getter" methods. (See below "Sending messages")

Instantiation (creating an object)

Once the class and its constructor have been defined, and each of the methods coded, we can start creating and naming actual objects. The creation of a new object (an instance of a class) is known as **instantiation**. Multiple instances of a class can be created which each share identical methods and attributes, but the values of those attributes will be unique to each instance.

This means that multiple enemy objects (zombies, for example) can be created in a computer game by programming just one zombie class, with health, position and speed attributes; but each individual zombie could operate independently with different attribute values.

Suppose we want to create a new stock item called book1. The type of variable to assign to book1 has to be stated. This will be the class name, StockItem. The word new is typically used (e.g. in Java) to **instantiate** (create) a new object in the class.

```
book1 = new StockItem("PT123", "Book", "Computer Science", 35)
```

book1 is called **a reference type variable**, or simply a **reference variable**. Note that this is a different type of variable from stockID or qtyInStock, which are String or Integer variables.

Like primitive variables of type integer, double, char (and the special case String), reference variables are named memory locations in which you can store information. However, a reference variable does not hold the object – it holds a pointer or reference to where the object itself is stored.

A **variable reference diagram** shows in graphical form the new StockItem object referenced by the variable book1. In the diagram, reference variables are shown as circles and primitive data types (and string variables) are shown as rectangles.

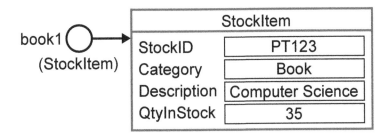

12-67

Sending messages

Messages can be categorised as either "getter" or "setter" messages. In some languages, "getter" messages are written as **functions** which return an answer, and "setter" messages as **procedures** which change the state of an object. This is reflected in the pseudocode used in this book.

The state of an object can be examined or changed by sending it a message, for example to get or increase the quantity in stock. To get the quantity in stock of book1, for example, you could write:

```
quantity ← book1.GetQtyInStock
```

To record the sale of 3 book1 objects, you could write

```
book1.SellStock(3)
```

Q2: Complete the class definition for `Radio` shown in the figure below. Include the instance variables and appropriate method headers written as functions or procedures.

```
Radio = Class
    Public
        Procedure SetVolume(Integer aVolume)
        Function GetVolume
        * insert more methods here
    * instance variables
    Private
        Volume: Integer
        * insert more instance variables here
```

Write pseudocode to instantiate two new radio objects named `robertsRadio` and `philipsRadio`.

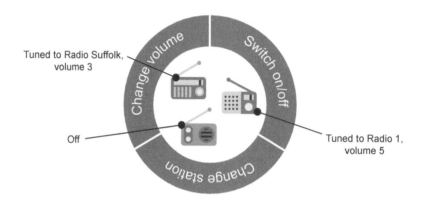

A radio modelled as a software object

Each object belongs to a class, and all the objects in the same class have the same structure and methods but they each have their own data. Objects created from a class are called **instances** of the class.

Q3: Draw a variable reference diagram to show the two new radio objects.

Encapsulation

An object **encapsulates** both its state (the values of its instance variables) and its behaviours or methods. All the data and methods of each object are wrapped up into a single entity so that the attributes and behaviours of one object cannot affect the way in which another object functions. For example, setting the `volume` of the `philipsRadio` object to 5 has no effect on any other `radio` object.

Encapsulation is a fundamental principle of object-oriented programming and is very powerful. It means, for example, that in a large project different programmers can work on different classes and not have to worry about how other parts of the system may affect any code they write. They can also use methods from other classes without having to know how they work.

Related to encapsulation is the concept of **information hiding**, whereby details of an object's instance variables are hidden so that other objects must use messages to interact with that object's state.

To invoke the method `ReceiveStock`, for example, we might write:

```
book1.ReceiveStock(50);
```

12-67

This would have the effect of updating the quantity in stock of book1 by 50. A programmer using the method does not need to know how this is achieved. The documentation of each method will specify the number and variable type of any arguments that need to be passed to the method, and what value, if any, is returned by the method.

Q4: Write statements to invoke the procedures to switch on the philipsRadio, and tune the robertsRadio to BBC2.

Inheritance

Classes can **inherit** data and behaviour from a parent class in much the same way that children can inherit characteristics from their parents. A "child" class in object-oriented program is referred to as a **subclass**, and a "parent" class as a **superclass**.

For example, we could draw an inheritance hierarchy for animals that feature in a computer game. Note that the inheritance relationship in the corresponding **inheritance diagram** is shown by an unfilled arrow at the "parent" end of the relationship.

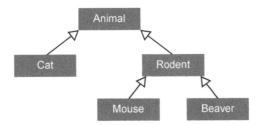

Class diagram involving inheritance

12-67

All the animals in the superclass Animal share common attributes such as colour and position. Animals may also have common procedures (methods), such as moveLeft, moveRight. A Cat may have an extra attribute hungry, and an extra method pounce. A Rodent may have an extra method gnaw. A Beaver has an extra method, makeDam.

Q5: What extra methods might Mouse have?

When to use inheritance

There is a simple rule to determine whether inheritance is appropriate in a program, called the "**is a**" rule, which requires an object to have a relationship to another object before it can inherit from the object. This rule asks, in effect, "Is object A an object B"? For example, "Is a Cat an Animal?" "Is a Mouse a Rodent?" Technically, there is nothing to stop you coding a program in which a man inherits the attributes and methods of a mouse, but this is going to cause confusion for users!

Coding inherited classes

Common behaviour can be defined in a **superclass** and inherited into a **subclass**.

To code the class header for Cat, which is a subclass of Animal, in pseudocode we could write something like

```
Cat = Subclass(Animal) or
Class Cat(Animal)
```

or in Java, for example,

```
public class Cat extends Animal
```

Q6: Complete the following pseudocode class definitions for `Animal`, `Rodent` and `Beaver`.

An `Animal` has methods `MoveLeft`, `MoveRight` and attributes `Colour` and `Position`

A `Rodent` has an additional method `Gnaw`

A `Beaver` has additional methods `CutTree`, `MakeDam` and additional attributes `TreesCut`, `DamComplete`

```
Animal = Class
    Public
        Procedure MoveLeft(Integer Steps)
        insert code  for procedures
        Function GetPosition
        insert functions
    Private
        Position: Integer
        insert attributes


Rodent = Subclass(Animal)
    Public
```

Exercises

1. A sports club keeps details of its members. Each member has a unique membership number, first name, surname and telephone number recorded. Three classes have been identified:

```
Member
JuniorMember
SeniorMember
```

The classes `JuniorMember` and `SeniorMember` are related, by single inheritance, to the class `Member`.

(a) Draw an inheritance diagram for the given classes. [2]

(b) Programs that use objects of the class `Member` need to add a new member's details, delete a member's details, and show a member's details. No other form of access is to be allowed.

Complete the class definition for this class.

```
Member = Class



End
```
[4]

(c) In object-oriented programming, what is meant by **encapsulation**? [1]

2. (a) In an object-oriented computer game there is a class called `Crawlers`. Two sub-classes of `Crawlers` are `Spiders` and `Bugs`. Draw an inheritance diagram for this. [2]

(b) For the sub-class `Spiders` suggest:

(i) **one** property;

(ii) **one** method. [2]

Chapter 68 – Object-oriented design principles

Objectives

- Understand concepts of association, composition and aggregation
- Understand the use of polymorphism and overriding
- Be aware of object-oriented design principles:
  - encapsulate what varies
  - favour composition over inheritance
  - program to interfaces, not implementation
- Be able to draw and interpret class diagrams

Association, aggregation and composition

Recall that inheritance is based on an "is a" relationship between two classes. For example, a cat "is a(n)" animal, a car "is a" vehicle. In a similar fashion, **association** may be loosely described as a "**has a**" relationship between classes. Thus a railway company may be associated with the engines and carriages it owns, or the track that it maintains. A teacher may be associated with a form bi-directionally – a teacher "has a" student, and a student "has a" teacher. However, there is no **ownership** between objects and each has their own lifecycle, and can be created and deleted independently.

Association aggregation, or simply **aggregation**, is a special type of more specific association. It can occur when a class is a collection or container of other classes, but the contained classes do not have a strong lifecycle dependency on the container. For example, a player who is part of a team does not cease to exist if the team is disbanded.

Aggregation may be shown in class diagrams using a hollow diamond shape between the two classes.

Class diagram showing association aggregation

Composition aggregation, or simply **composition**, is a stronger form of aggregation. If the container is destroyed, every instance of the contained class is also destroyed. For example if a hotel is destroyed, every room in the hotel is destroyed.

Composition may be shown in class diagrams using a filled diamond shape. The diamond is at the end of the class that owns the creational responsibility.

Class diagram showing composition aggregation

Q1: Specify whether each of the following describe **association aggregation** or **composition aggregation**.

(a) Zoo and ZooAnimal

(b) RaceTrack and TrackSection

(c) Department and Teacher

12-68

Polymorphism

Polymorphism refers to a programming language's ability to process objects differently depending on their class. For example, in the last chapter we looked at an application that had a superclass `Animal`, and subclasses `Cat` and `Rodent`. All objects in subclasses of `Animal` can execute the methods `moveLeft`, `moveRight`, which will cause the animal to move one space left or right.

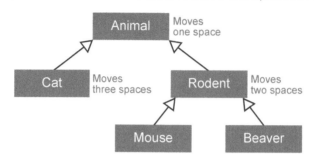

We might decide that a `cat` should move three spaces when a `moveLeft` or `moveRight` message is received, and a `Rodent` should move two spaces. We can define different methods within each of the classes to implement these moves, but keep the same method name for each class.

Defining a method with the same name and formal argument types as a method inherited from a superclass is called **overriding**. In the example above, the `moveLeft` method in each of the `Cat` and `Rodent` classes overrides the method in the superclass `Animal`.

12-68

> **Q2:** Suppose that `tom` is an instance of the `Cat` class, and `jerry` is an instance of the `Mouse` class. What will happen when each of these statements is executed?
>
> tom.moveRight()
>
> jerry.moveRight()
>
> **Q3:** Looking at the diagram above, what changes do you need to make so that `bertie`, an instance of the `Beaver` class, moves only one space when given a `moveRight()` message?

Class definition including override

Class definitions for the classes `Animal` and `Cat` will be something like this:

```
Animal = Class
        Public
            Procedure moveLeft
            Procedure moveRight
        Protected
            Position: Integer
        End
Cat = Subclass (Animal)
        Public
            Procedure moveLeft (Override)
            Procedure moveRight (Override)
            Procedure pounce
        Private
            Name: String
        End
```

Note: The 'Protected' access modifier is described on page 356.

"Favour composition over inheritance"

Composition is generally considered preferable to inheritance for implementing the desired functionality of a system. The main reason for this is that it allows greater flexibility, because composition is a less rigid relationship between two objects than that between two objects with an inheritance relationship. Also, in some cases, an object may be composed of several other objects but cannot be said in a real-world sense to "inherit" their characteristics.

For example, suppose a class house has walls, windows and a door.

We can define classes for House, Wall, Door, Window and Roof. Each of these classes will need attributes of height, width and colour. The House class will need attributes Wall, Door, Window, Roof and a method to draw and position the house.

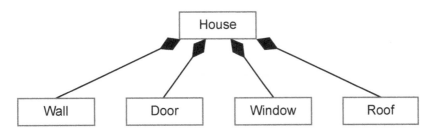

Class diagram showing composition aggregation

The class definition for the House and Wall classes will be written in pseudocode something like this, with similar definitions for Door, Window and Roof.

```
House = Class
    Public
        Procedure drawHouse
        Procedure setHousePosition
        Procedure getHousePosition
    Private
        TheWall: Wall
        TheDoor: Door
        WindowLeft: Window
        WindowRight: Window
        TheRoof: Roof
    End
Wall = Class
    Public
        Procedure drawWall
    Private
        WallHeight: Real
        WallWidth: Real
        WallColour: Integer
    End
```

12-68

Public, private and protected access modifiers (specifiers)

Related to encapsulation is the concept of **information hiding**, meaning that an object's instance variables (e.g. wall, door, etc. in the above example) are hidden so that other objects must use messages (i.e. invoke a procedure or function) to interact with that object's state. (Compare this with the use of local variables in subroutines in a procedural language.) The access modifiers **public**, **private** and **protected** are included in a class definition to implement data hiding.

- If a method or instance variable is declared **private**, only code within the class itself can access it.

- If a method or instance variable is declared **public**, code within any class can access it.

Most commonly, instance variables are declared private and methods public, so that other classes cannot change the values of variables in another class but they can use their methods.

There is a third specifier, **protected**, the definition of which varies between languages. In some languages this restricts access to members of a subclass, in others to members in the same package or library of classes. For example, the classes `Rectangle`, `Triangle`, `Circle` etc. may all be part of a `Shapes` package.

The table below summarises the three types of access modifier.

Member is accessible...	Public	Protected	Private
Within the defining class	Yes	Yes	Yes
Via inheritance	Yes	Yes	No
Via a reference to an object of the class	Yes	Only if it is in a subclass/in the same package (definition varies between languages)	No

Class diagram with access specifiers

Example 1

Animal is an abstract class, with methods that are overridden in the Bird and Mammal classes. It is not possible to create an Animal object.

The class diagram below shows inheritance, with private (-) and public (+) specifiers. (A protected specifier would be shown with #.)

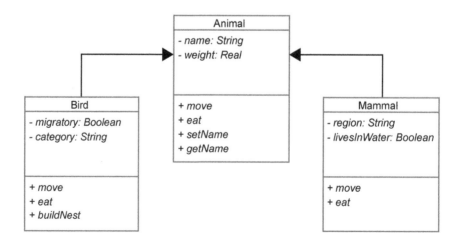

Programming to an interface

In many situations, a number of different classes of object all need to understand a particular set of messages even though there is no relationship between them. A simple set of messages `switchOn` and `setTimer` could be sent to a wide variety of objects such as `microwave`, `lamp`, `oven`, `watch` etc. How each object responds to the message will vary depending on their class.

In this context, an **interface** is a collection of abstract methods that a group of unrelated classes may implement. Although the methods are specified in the interface, they will only be implemented by a class that implements the interface, and not in the interface itself. The programmer constructing the list of messages or methods does not need to know how the instances of objects in each class will respond to each message.

The programming will be something like this:

```
Public interface Switches
    Procedure SwitchOn
    Procedure SwitchOff
    Procedure SetTimer(aTime)
    Function GetTimer
    etc
End
```

A programmer who wants class `Microwave` to implement the `Switches` interface then includes the name of the interface in the class header:

```
Class Microwave implements Switches
```

The objects in class microwave must be able to receive messages `SwitchOn`, `SetTimer`, etc.

Objects in a class implementing an interface must be able to receive all the messages corresponding to the methods listed in the interface. One advantage of using such an interface is that new classes can be added which use the interface without in any way affecting existing classes.

Encapsulate what varies

The strategy of **encapsulating what varies** is used in order to reduce maintenance and testing effort. It means that when something changes in a program, (such as different specifications for reserving library books or calculating customer discounts in an online store) if the concept in question is encapsulated in a single module, only that module will need to change. At the design stage, consideration should be given to requirements that are most likely to change in the future. It is these aspects of the system that are most important to encapsulate so that if they are changed in the future, the overall amount of code that needs to be modified is minimised.

Furthermore, if a module for calculating customer discounts, for example, contains code for checking a customer's credit status, all that code could itself be encapsulated in a separate module.

Using an interface class encapsulating the varying concept is one way of implementing this concept, since the interface is implemented differently by different classes and code that relies on the interface can handle any class implementing the interface. Thus for example if a different type of electronic gadget is introduced which uses a different procedure to switch on and off, a new module can be introduced and no other module needs to change.

12-68

Advantages of the object-oriented paradigm

Building code into objects has a number of advantages, including:

- The object-oriented methodology forces designers to go through an extensive planning phase, which makes for better designs with fewer weaknesses.

- Encapsulation: the source code for an object can be written, tested and maintained independently of the code for other objects

- Once an object is created, knowledge of how its methods are implemented is not necessary in order for a programmer to use it.

- New objects can easily be created with small differences to existing ones

- Re-usability: objects that are already defined, coded and tested may be used in many different programs. OOP provides a good framework for code libraries with a range of software components that can easily be adapted by a programmer.

- Software maintenance: an object oriented program is much easier to maintain than one written in a procedural language because of its rigidly enforced modular structure.

Exercises

12-68

1. An object-oriented program is being written to store details of and play digital media files that are stored on a computer. A class **MediaFile** has been created and two subclasses, **VideoFile** and **MusicFile** are to be developed.

   The classes **VideoFile** and MusicFile are related to **MediaFile** by single inheritance.

   (a) Explain what is meant by *inheritance*. [1]

   (b) Draw an inheritance diagram for the three classes. [2]

   (c) One important feature of an object-oriented programming language is the facility to override methods (functions and procedures).

   Explain what is meant by *overriding* when writing programs that involve inheritance. [2]

   (d) The **MediaFile** class has data fields **Title** and **Duration**.

   The class definition for **MediaFile** is:

   ```
   MediaFile = Class
      Public
         Procedure PlayFile
         Function GetTitle
         Function GetDuration
      Private
         Title: String
         Duration: Real
   End
   ```

   Note that the class does not have procedures to set the values of the variables as these are read automatically from data stored within the actual media file.

   The **MusicFile** class has the following additional data fields:

   - **Artist**: Stores the name of the band or singer that recorded the music.

   - **SampleRate**: Stores the rate at which the music has been sampled

   - **BitDepth**: Stores the number of bits in which each sampled value is represented.

   Write the class definition for **MusicFile**. [4]

AQA Unit 3 Qu 11 June 2010

2. (a) In object-oriented programming, what is meant by **polymorphism**? [2]

(b) An object-oriented program stores details of a class `Bird` and a subclass `Seagull`, defined as follows:

```
Class Bird
   Public
      Procedure move
         system.print("Birds can fly")
      End
End

Class Seabird extends Bird
   Public
      Procedure move (override)
         system.print("Seabirds can fly and swim")
      End
End
```

Two new objects are instantiated with the lines:

```
Bird bird1 = new Bird()
Bird bird2 = new Seabird()
```

(i) What will be printed when the following lines are executed?

```
bird1.move
bird2.move
```
[2]

(ii) Explain your answer. [2]

3. (a) In object-oriented programming, what is meant by **aggregation**? [1]

(b) An object-oriented program has been written for a company selling garden furniture. The furniture includes tables, chairs and sets of furniture which include a table and several chairs.

Draw a class diagram for the classes `Table`, `Chair`, `GardenSet`. [2]

(c) Some instance variables (fields) required for the `GardenSet` class are

    `TableType, ChairType, NumberOfChairs`

A method required for the `GardenSet` class is

    `DisplayDetails`

The instance variables are declared as `Private`, and the method `Public`.

Explain the effect of the access modifiers `Private` and `Public`. Why is it common to make instance variables `Private` and methods `Public`? [3]

12-68

Chapter 69 – Functional programming

Objectives

- Understand what is meant by a programming paradigm
- Define function type, domain and co-domain
- Understand what is meant by a first-class object and how such an object may be used
- Be able to evaluate simple functions
- Use functional composition to combine two functions

Programming paradigms

A **programming paradigm** is a style of computer programming. Different programming languages support tackling problems in different ways, and there are four major programming paradigms or types of language:

- **Procedural** languages such as Python or Pascal, which have a series of instructions that tell the computer what to do with the input in order to solve the problem

- **Object-oriented** languages such as Java. Python and Delphi also support object-oriented programming

- **Declarative** languages such as SQL, where you write statements that describe the problem to be solved, and the language implementation decides the best way of solving it

- **Functional** programming languages such as Haskell, or languages such as Python, C# and Java which also support functional programming techniques. In a functional program, functions, not objects or procedures, are used as the fundamental building blocks of a program. Statements are written as a series of functions which accept input data as arguments and return an output.

What is a function?

A function is a mapping from a set of inputs, called the **domain**, to a set of possible outputs, known as the **co-domain**.

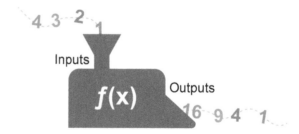

The function machine illustrated above could be defined in more mathematical terms as:

$$f: A \rightarrow B \text{ where } f(x) = x^2$$

That is to say that the *input in domain A produces output in co-domain B*.

The domain and co-domain are always subsets of objects in some data type. In the above function, we could define the domain A as the set of integers, for example. The co-domain B is then the set of all positive integers that are greater than or equal to zero.

> **Q1:** A function f is defined as f: A → B where f(x) = x^2 + 5. The domain A is the set of all real numbers. What is the co-domain B?

A function does not have to be an algebraic formula. For example, we could map names to ID numbers using a function:

f: {Ben, Anna, Michael, Gerri} → {34, 26, 74, 12}

Ben maps to 34, Anna to 26 and so on. Notice that the domain and co-domain are of different data types.

Functional programming in Haskell

Haskell is a functional programming language which will be useful for gaining some practical experience in functional programming. If you want to do some practical work in Haskell to accompany the theory in the next three chapters, you will need access to a text editor such as Notepad for writing programs, and the Haskell platform which uses GHC (**G**lasgow **H**askell **C**ompiler) for compiling your programs. This is available free from https://www.haskell.org/platform.

Once Haskell is installed, you can compile and run a program which you have saved, or use the interactive mode which allows you to type in a function and apply it directly by passing it appropriate **parameters** or **arguments**.

Note that the terms *parameter* and *argument* are often used interchangeably, though the distinction can be made that an *argument* is a value or expression passed to a function, and a *parameter* is a reference declared in a function declaration.

Haskell notation is used in these chapters, and instructions for running each program from a script or in interactive mode are given as each new statement is introduced. If you are not using Haskell, you will still be able to grasp the general principles of functional programming.

12-69

Starting Haskell

We will use a text editor to write a simple program consisting of one function.

- Open Notepad or any other text editor and type the following lines:

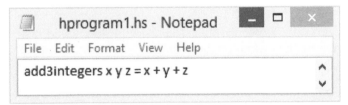

Notice that the function name, `add3integers`, is followed by its three parameters `x` `y` `z` separated by spaces. No parentheses or commas are used in Haskell, unlike in, for example, Python or Visual Basic.

- Save this program as `hprogram1.hs` in a convenient folder.

- Now load Haskell (the program name is WinGCHi.exe)

- In the Haskell window, use the file menu to navigate to your folder and load the file `hprogram1.hs`

- The prompt changes from `Prelude>` to `*Main>`

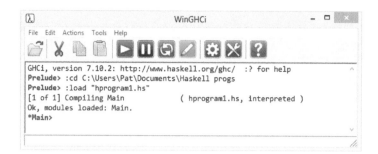

Function application

The process of giving particular inputs to a function is known as **function application**.

We can **apply** or **call** the function `add3integers` to find the sum of three integers 5, 6 and 7 by writing

```
add3integers 5 6 7
```

The function name is followed by the parameters, separated by spaces.

The result, 18, will be displayed.

The type of the function is *f: integer x integer → integer* where *integer x integer* is the Cartesian product of the set integer with itself. (Spoken *integer cross integer maps to integer* – See Chapter 51.)

Instead of typing function definitions into a text document, saving and loading the program, we can type function definitions directly in the Haskell window in interactive mode. The function definition must be preceded by the word `let` in interactive mode or Haskell will give an error message.

12-69

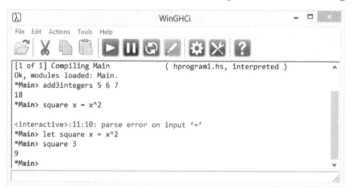

> **Q2:** What do you think the following function does?
>
> ```
> product x y z = x * y * z
> ```
>
> Apply the function to find the product of 2, 3 and 4. What are the parameters of the function?
>
> **Q3:** Write a function called sumOfSquares which calculates the sum of the squares of two numbers. Apply the function to calculate the sum of the squares of 3 and 4. (Use the notation x^2 for x^2.)

First-class objects

In a functional programming language, a **first-class object** is an object which may:

- appear in expressions
- be assigned to a variable
- be assigned as an argument
- be returned in a function call

For example, integers, floating point values, characters and strings are first-class objects. **Functions** are also first-class objects so may themselves be passed as arguments.

What's special about functional programming languages?

There are some major differences between procedural and functional programming languages. The importance and significance of these features will become apparent when you reach the chapter on Big Data. Here are some of these features listed and explained.

Statelessness

When you execute a procedural program such as Python or Pascal, the computer's memory changes state as it goes along. You could execute the following statements, for example:

```
x = 5
x = x + 1
```

In a functional programming language, the value of a variable cannot change. Variables are said to be **immutable**, and the program is said to be **stateless**.

Try this out now. In Notepad or any text editor, type the following lines:

```
a = 4
a = 5
b = 10
addTwoNumbers x y = x + y
```

Save this program as `variables.hs`, and try to load it. You will get an error message:

```
Prelude> :load "variables.hs"
[1 of 1] Compiling Main            ( variables.hs, interpreted )

variables.hs:2:1:
    Multiple declarations of 'a'
    Declared at: variables.hs:1:1
                 variables.hs:2:1
Failed, modules loaded: none.
Prelude>
```

Remove the second assignment statement a = 5 from the program, save and reload. This time it should load with no problem. Now try typing `addTwoNumbers a b`.

No side effects

The only thing a function can do is calculate something and return a result, and it is said to have no **side effects**.

A consequence of not being able to change the value of an object is that a function that is called twice with the same parameters will always return the same result. This is called **referential transparency** and makes it relatively easy for programmers to write correct, bug-free programs. A simple function can be proved to be correct, and then more complex functions can be built using these functions.

Try this out by adding some more lines to your program `variables.hs` as shown:

```
a = 4
b = 10
addTwoNumbers x y = x + y
doubleSmallNumber x = if x < 10
                        then x * 2
                        else x
```

12-69

363

Save and load the program.

Notice that we have used an IF statement in the function `doubleSmallNumber`. An IF statement in Haskell must include an ELSE clause. Try out the functions in Haskell:

```
Prelude> :load "variables.hs"
[1 of 1] Compiling Main              ( variables.hs, interpreted )
Ok, modules loaded: Main.
*Main> addTwoNumbers a b
14
*Main> doubleSmallNumber a
8
*Main> doubleSmallNumber b
10
```

Now try using a function as an argument:

```
*Main> addTwoNumbers (doubleSmallNumber a) b
18
```

You can even use a function in the definition of a new function. Add the following function to your program `variables.hs` in the text editor, save and load.

```
addAndDouble x y = addTwoNumbers (doubleSmallNumber x) y
```

Q4: What will be the result returned by applying the function with the following parameters:

(a)   a, b

(b)   5, 20

(c)   20, 5

12-69

Composition of functions

Since a function may be used as an argument, we can combine two functions to get a new function. This is called **functional composition**.

Given two functions

    f: A → B and g: B → C

the function **g** o **f** (called *the composition of f and g*) is a function whose domain is A and co-domain is C.

Example 1

Consider the two functions $f(x) = x + 3$ and $g(x) = 2x^2$

    g o **f** could be written as $g(f(x)) = g(x+3) = 2 (x+3)^2$

f is applied first and then g is applied to the result returned by f.

In Haskell notation, we would write

    f x = x + 3   (f)

    g x = 2 * x^2   (g)

Applying the function g(f(x)) or **g** o **f** with argument 4, in Haskell we write

    (g.f) 4

which will return the value 98, since $f(4) = 7$, $g(7) = 2*49 = 98$

    (f.g) 4 will return the value 35, since $g(4) = 32$, $f(32) = 32 + 3 = 35$

Q5: What value will be returned if we apply the function with the following statement?

(g.f) 5

Q6: Using Haskell notation write two functions f(a) = a + 1 and g(a) = a³. What will be the value of each of these functions if a = 4? Write a statement to evaluate the composition of g and f, i.e. **g** o **f** when passed the argument 4.

Q7: The function **doubleNum** is defined as `doubleNum x = 2 * x`. Write a function **quadruple** which uses the function **doubleNum** in its definition.

Types and typeclasses

In Haskell, **types** are sets of values, and **typeclasses** are sets of types. So for example:

Type `Integer` includes values 1, 2, 3 ...

Type `Float` includes 3.142, 2.5

Type `Bool` includes True and False

Type `Char` includes a, b, c ...

Bool

Char

`Integer`, `Int`, `Double` and `Float` are all in Typeclass `Num`. `Integer` is unbounded to represent really big numbers. `Int` is restricted to minimum and maximum value.

Note that Type and Typeclass names always start with uppercase letters.

Functions also have types. It is considered good practice to always give functions explicit type declarations. These take the form shown in the example below (colour coded to show the relationship between the declaration and the function arguments):

`sumOfSquares :: Integer -> Integer -> Integer`

sumOfSquares x y = x^2 + y^2

The types of the two arguments x and y are both declared as integer, and the result is also an integer. The three types are written one after the other separated by ->.

The value returned by a function does not necessarily have the same type as the arguments. For example, the function `isEqual x y = x == y` will return `True` if x and y are equal, `false` otherwise. Note the **equality operator** `==` used here.

`isEqual :: Int -> Int -> Bool`
`isEqual x y = x == y`

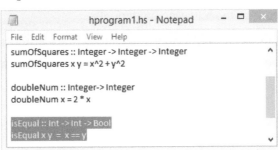

12-69

To try this out – type the statements as shown in the screenshot above into your text editor, save the file and load it again using **File, Load...** from the menu.

You can check the function type in Haskell by typing

:type isEqual *or*

:t isEqual

```
*Main> isEqual 4 5
False
*Main> :t isEqual
isEqual :: Int -> Int -> Bool
```

Q8: A function cuboidVol takes 3 arguments l, b, h representing the length, breadth and height of a cuboid as floating point numbers (real) numbers of type `Float`. Write a type statement followed by the function definition. What will be returned if the function is applied to parameters 4, 2, 0.5?

Type variables

Using interactive mode in Haskell, you may see something like the following:

```
*Main> let sumOfTwo x y = x + y
*Main> sumOfTwo 2 3
5
*Main> :t sumOfTwo
sumOfTwo :: Num a => a -> a -> a
```

Here, no type declaration has been written, and Haskell cannot tell what the variable types are – they could be Integer or Float, for example. As shown by the fact that it does not begin with an uppercase letter, a is neither a type nor a typeclass; it is in fact a **type variable**, which represents any type.

Exercises

1. (a) Use functional programming notation to write a type declaration and define a function

$$f(x) = 2x + 1$$

Assume all values are integers, and name the function `doublePlusOne`. [4]

   (b) Write a second function named `square` which returns the value of $g(x) = x^2$. [2]

   (c) Combine the two functions in **(a)** and **(b)** to write a function $h(x)$ which returns the value of

$$h(x) = g(x) + f(x)$$

Name the function `squarexPlusf`. What will be returned when this function is applied to the parameter 3? [3]

2. (a) Explain what is meant by the following statements:

   (i) "In a functional programming language, variables are **immutable**." [1]

   (ii) "Functional programming is **stateless**, and has **no side effects**." [2]

   (b) Explain why these features help programmers to create programs that do not contain hard-to-find bugs. [3]

Chapter 70 – Function application

Objectives

- Understand what is meant by partial function application
- Know that a function takes only one argument which may itself be a function
- Define and use higher-order functions, including map, filter and fold

Higher-order functions

A **higher-order function** is one which either takes a function as an argument or returns a function as a result, or both. The function described in the previous chapter was an example of a higher order function which took the function `doubleSmallNumber x` as an argument :

```
addAndDouble x y = addTwoNumbers (doubleSmallNumber x) y
```

Every function in Haskell takes only one argument. This may seem like a contradiction because we have seen many functions such as the one above, or the one below, which adds three integers,

```
add3Integers x y z = x + y + z
```

which appear to take several arguments. So how can this be true?

Any function takes only one parameter at a time

Taken at face value and assuming the function takes three integer parameters and returns an integer result, the type declaration for this function would normally be written

```
add3Integers :: integer -> integer -> integer -> integer
```

It could also be written

```
add3Integers :: integer -> (integer -> (integer -> integer))
```

How the function is evaluated

What happens when you write `add3Integers 2 4 5`?

The function `add3Integers` is applied to the arguments. It takes the first argument 2 and produces a new function (shown in blue above) which will add 2 to its arguments, 4 and 5.

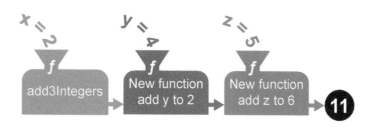

This function (shown in blue) produces a new function (shown in green) that takes the argument 5 and adds it to 6, returning the result, 11.

Our function `add3Integers` takes an integer argument (2) and returns a function of type

```
(integer -> (integer -> integer))
```

This function takes an integer argument (4) and returns a function of type `(integer -> integer)`

This function takes an integer argument (5) and returns an integer (11).

Partial function application

Partial function application takes advantage of this by decomposing multi-argument functions into smaller functions with fewer arguments. For example, suppose we have a function `add` that takes two integers and returns their sum:

```
add :: Integer -> Integer -> Integer
add x y = x + y
```

Remember that `add 3 4` actually means `(add 3) 4`. If we write

```
add 3
```

we will get an error message from Haskell saying it doesn't know how to print the resulting value, which is a function of type `Integer -> Integer`.

However, we can now use this partially applied function as an argument of a different function – `addSix`, for example, adds six to the result of the function.

```
addSix :: Integer -> Integer
addSix = add 6
```

We can now use this function, and it adds 6 to the n that replaces `add` in the calling statement.

```
*Main> addSix 10
16
```

We have a function `add` that takes more than one argument, and we pass it fewer arguments than it wants. It returns a new function that will take the remaining argument and return the result, as demonstrated with the `addSix` function.

Partial application means fixing/binding the values of some inputs to a function to produce another more specific function.

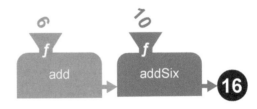

Q1: What will be returned by the following function call?

```
addSix 3
```

Now consider the following code snippet which uses the function add3Integers that we defined earlier. This function takes three arguments.

```
*Main> let addTen = add3Integers 10
*Main> addTen 1 2
13
*Main> addTen 7 8
25
```

Once again we have created a brand new function "on the fly" by using **partial function application**. We have passed two arguments instead of three to add3Integers and the third argument is supplied by `addTen`.

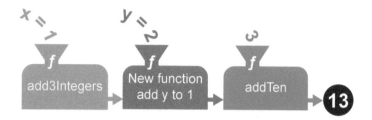

The function `add3Integers` is partially applied to the arguments 1 and 2, giving 3, and the resulting function is applied to 10.

Q2: What is returned as a result of executing the following statements?

```
add3Integers :: Integer -> Integer -> Integer -> Integer
add3Integers x y z = x + y + z
addTen :: Integer -> Integer -> Integer
addTen = add3Integers 10
addTen 40 50
```

12-70

Map

Map is a higher-order function that takes a list and the function to be applied to the elements in the list as inputs, and returns a list made by applying the function to each element of the old list.

Lists will be covered in detail in the next chapter, but for now it is enough to know that a list is a collection of elements which can be written in square brackets, e.g. [3, 7, 5, 9]. The empty list is written [].

The function `max  x  y` is a built-in library function which returns the maximum of two numbers:

e.g.   `max  8  3` will return 8.

We can partially apply `max` to get the maximum of 3 and its argument. We then map that function, which has no name, to a list:

    map (max 3) [1,2,3,4,5].

getting the result

    [3,3,3,4,5]

Here, `max` has been applied to each element of the list in turn. The maximum of 3 and 1 is 3, so the first element of the resulting list is 3. Likewise, the maximum of 2 and 3 is 3, so the second element of the resulting list is 3, and so on.

Here's another example:

    map (+5) [2,8,4,10]

This returns

    [7,13,9,15]

Filter

Filter is another higher-order function which takes a **predicate** (to define a Boolean condition) and a list. This returns the elements within the list that satisfy the Boolean condition.

e.g. `filter (>6)[2,5,6,8,9]`

will return

`[8,9]`

You can write your own predicate to be used in the filter:

e.g. `isEven n = n 'mod' 2 == 0`

(Use the backward quotes on the left of the 1 key on the keyboard to surround the mod operator.)

`filter (isEven)[1,2,3,4,5,6]`

will return `[2,4,6]`

Fold (reduce) function

A fold function reduces a list to a single value, using recursion. For example, to find the sum of all the elements of a list, we write:

`foldl (+) 0 [2, 3, 4, 5]`

this will return the value 14. The initial value 0 is combined with the first element of the list, which is then recursively combined with the first element of the remaining list, and so on. This could be parenthesised as

`(((0 + 2) + 3) + 4) + 5`

(`foldl` stands for fold left, i.e. the recursion starts with the leftmost value. `foldr` or fold right starts with the rightmost value. In this example it would not make any difference which we used.)

Exercises

1. The function `multiply3` is defined as follows:

```
multiply3 :: Integer -> Integer -> Integer -> Integer
multiply3 x y z = x * y * z
```

(a)   What result is returned by the following statement?

`multiply3 2 3 5`   [1]

(b)   A further function `multByTen` is defined as follows:

`multByTen = multiply3 10`

(i)   What result is returned by the following statement?

`multByTen 6 2`   [1]

(ii)   What is partial function application? Explain, in terms of partial function application, how this result is arrived at.   [3]

2. (a) Explain what the `map` function does in a functional programming language such as Haskell.   [2]

(b) Use `map` to write a function that trebles each element of the list `[1,2,3,4,5]`   [2]

3. Write statements that will return a list containing only the odd numbers from the list.   [3]

12-70

Chapter 71 – Lists in functional programming

Objectives

- Understand that a list is a concatenation of a head and a tail, where the head is an element of a list and the tail is a list

- Define an empty list

- Describe and apply the following operations:
  - return head of list
  - return tail of list
  - test for empty list
  - return length of list
  - construct an empty list
  - prepend an item to a list
  - append an item to a list

Head and tail of a list

A **list** is a collection of elements of a similar type, such as integers, characters or strings, enclosed in square brackets. For example, in Haskell a list may be created using the keyword **let**:

```
let names = ["Anna", "Bob", "Jo", "Keira", "Tom", "George"]
let numbers = [3, 7, 14, 83, 2, 77]
```

(Alternatively, you can create the list in Notepad, save and load the file.

```
lists.hs - Notepad                                    —    □    ✕
File   Edit   Format   View   Help
names = ["Anna", "Bob", "Jo", "Keira", "Tom", "George"]    ^
numbers = [3, 7, 14, 83, 2, 77]
```

A list is composed of a **head** and a **tail**. The head is the first element of the list, and the tail is the remainder of the list. In Haskell:

```
Prelude> :load "lists.hs"
[1 of 1] Compiling Main ( lists.hs, interpreted )
Ok, modules loaded: Main.
*Main> names
["Anna","Bob","Jo","Keira","Tom","George"]
*Main> numbers
[3,7,14,83,2,77]
*Main> head names
"Anna"
*Main> tail names
["Bob","Jo","Keira","Tom","George"]
```

Q1: What is the head of the list `numbers`? What is the tail of this list?

We can apply the list argument repeatedly to the function tail. For example:

12-71

```
*Main> tail (tail (tail numbers))
[83,2,77]
```

Working from the right, the tail of the list [3, 7, 14, 83, 2, 77] is [7,14,83,2,77]

The tail of this list is [14, 83, 2, 77]

Finally the tail of this list is [83, 2, 77]

> **Q2:** Write a statement which applies the operation `tail` to the list `names` repeatedly until the list consists of a single element.

Note that applying a function such as `head` or `tail` does not change the original list. Lists are **immutable**, which means that they can never be changed.

Defining an empty list

An empty list has no elements and is written []. You can create an empty list directly in Haskell:

```
let newlist = []
```

The function **null** tests for an empty list.

```
*Main> null numbers
False
*Main> null newlist
True
*Main>
```

Prepending and appending to a list

Prepending means adding an element to the front of a list, and **appending** means adding an element to the end of a list.

To add an element to the front of the list, you can either add an element using the : (colon) operator, or add a list using the ++ operator.

```
*Main> 5:numbers
[5, 3, 7, 14, 83, 2, 77]
*Main> [6, 10] ++ numbers
[6, 10, 3, 7, 14, 83, 2, 77]
*Main> 8 : 9 : 10 : numbers
[8, 9, 10, 3, 7, 14, 83, 2, 77]
```

To append an element to the end of a list, one method in Haskell to use the ++ operator and append a list made from the element to be appended.

```
*Main> numbers ++ [100]
[3, 7, 14, 83, 2, 77, 100]
```

Remember this does not alter the original list. We can find the length of `numbers` using the `length` function.

```
*Main> length numbers
6
```

12-71

Q3: (a) Write code to create a new list [1,2,3,4] called newNumbers.

(b) Concatenate the two lists numbers and newNumbers; that is, create a new list called newList containing all the numbers from both lists.

(c) Use the filter function to obtain a list of all the numbers greater than 10 in the concatenated list.

(Tip: look back at the last chapter to remind yourself how the filter function works.)

Exercises

1. The list **animals** contains the following items:

["otter", "fox", "deer", "badger", "seal", "dolphin"]

What result is returned by each of the following function calls?

(a) tail animals [1]

(b) head (tail (tail animals)) [2]

(c) null (tail (tail (tail (tail (tail animals)))))) [2]

2. The list **results** contains the following items:

[56, 78, 45, 62, 68]

What result is returned by applying each of the following functions?

(a) map (*2) results [1]

(b) filter (>50) results [1]

(c) map (*2) (filter (>60) results) [2]

3. Write code to

(a) add the numbers 2, 6, 8 to the start of a list xs [7,2,4,10] [1]

(b) add the numbers 12,13,14 to the end of xs. [1]

(c) remove the first number from xs [1]

(d) replace the first two numbers from the list xs with 12, 13 [3]

12-71

Chapter 72 – Big Data

Objectives

- Understand that Big Data is a term used to describe data whose volume is too large to fit on a single server and is generally unstructured

- Describe examples of Big Data

- Describe features of functional programming which make it suitable for analysing Big Data

- Be familiar with the fact-based model for representing data

- Be familiar with graph schema for capturing the structure of the dataset

What is Big Data?

Big Data analysis is quite probably going to be the most exciting, interesting and useful field of study in the computing world over the next decade or two. We are just at the beginning of exploring its massive benefits in healthcare and medicine, business, communication, speech recognition, banking, and many other fields. Here are some questions it can answer:

- Does cellphone use increase the likelihood of cancer? With six billion cellphones in the world, there is plenty of data to analyse. (The answer turned out to be "No"!)

- How can you improve voice-translation software? By scoring the probability that a given digitised snippet of voice corresponds to a specific word. Google has made use of this data in its speech recognition software.

- How does the Bank of England find out whether house prices are rising or falling? By analysing search queries related to property.

- How can online education programmers use data collection to improve the courses offered? By studying data on the percentage of thousands of students registered who rewatched a segment of the course, suggesting it was not clear, or collecting data on wrong answers to assignments.

The term "Big Data" was first coined in the early 2000s by scientists working in fields such as astronomy and human genome projects, where the amount of data they were collecting was so massive that traditional methods of organising and analysing data, such as relational databases, could no longer be used. Initially, "Big Data" meant that the volume of data was so large that it could not fit into the memory of the computers that were used for processing it, so new tools were needed for analysing it.

Computer scientists and mathematicians soon realised that the most difficult aspect of Big Data was its lack of structure. The data cannot be neatly organised into the rows and columns of a relational database, and it is impossible to use standard query tools such as SQL. Frequently, it is essential to be able to analyse the data in seconds or milliseconds to produce a response.

These three aspects of Big Data can be summarised in terms of:

- **volume** – too big to fit on a single server

- **velocity** – milliseconds or seconds to respond, particularly with streamed data

- **variety** – the data may be in many forms such as structured, unstructured, text or multimedia

Essentially, Big Data collection and processing enables us to detect and analyse relationships within and among individual pieces of information that previously we were unable to grasp.

Examples of Big Data

Healthcare

Doctors and other medical professionals generally use two sets of data when diagnosing ailments and recommending treatments: retrospective data collected from the medical records not only of the patient but from thousands or millions of other people, and real-time clinical data such as blood pressure, temperature, etc. If for example a diabetic patient complains of numbness in their toes, the doctor can measure their blood flow, oxygen levels and so on, and from data gathered on a multitude of other patients with a similar problem, determine if this is a potentially serious situation and what treatment should be offered.

Recently, however, medical science has gone further and in many circumstances can take gene sequencing into account. Gene sequencing is already used to determine the best course of treatment for cancer patients, and as costs fall, it may become a routine part of a patient's medical record. In the case of an infectious disease outbreak, hours and even minutes matter in determining the best course of treatment for an individual patient.

But how much data is involved in sequencing one human genome? It depends on exactly what data is being collected for analysis, but assuming around three billion base pairs for a human genome, one estimate is around 200GB. Another estimate is that the human body contains about 150 trillion gigabytes of information… so there are undoubtedly challenges in analysing this type of data for an entire population!

Google

Google processes more than 24 petabytes of data per day – that's 24 x 10^{15} bytes of data. They receive more than three billion search queries every day and save every single one. The company can use this data in thousands of different ways. For example, between 2003 and 2008, Google computer scientists identified areas in the US affected by seasonal flu by what people searched for on the Internet. They did this by taking the 50 million most common search terms that Americans type and comparing them with the spread of seasonal flu between 2003 and 2008 and they found 45 search terms that when used together in a mathematical model, produced a strong correlation between their prediction and the official figures nationwide.

When a new flu virus called H1N1 struck in 2009, Google was able to identify its spread far more quickly than government statistics could, and thus arm public health officials with valuable information to contain the outbreak.

Amazon

The online bookseller Amazon uses the huge amounts of customer data that it collects to recommend specific books to its customers. In the early days of the company, they processed their data in a conventional way, by looking at topics and authors that the reader had purchased and recommending more of the same. This was generally more annoying than helpful to customers – if you have bought one book on Python programming, you don't necessarily need a recommendation for five more books on Python every time you log on.

What they then did was to apply Big Data techniques, simply finding associations among the products themselves, regardless of what a particular customer had bought. If huge numbers of customers who bought a book by Dan Brown also purchased a book by Ian McEwan, a customer who bought a book by one of those authors would be recommended a book by the other, even if they had never bought one before.

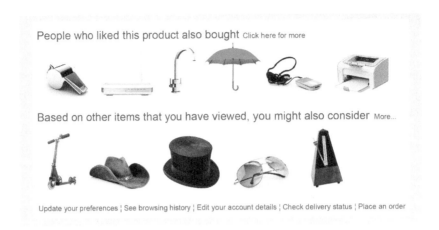

Personalised recommendations generated for users of online shopping websites

Functional programming and Big Data

Functional programming has features which make it useful for working with data distributed across several servers.

Writing correct code

- **Functional languages have no side effects**. A function is said to have a **side effect** if it modifies the state of the calling program in some way. For example, in a procedural language a particular function might modify a global variable, write to or delete data from a file. Functional languages support **statelessness**, meaning that the program's behaviour does not depend on how often a function is called or in what order different functions are called.

  This makes it easier to write correct code, and to understand and predict the behaviour of a program.

- **Functional programming languages support higher order functions.** A higher-order function is one which does at least one of the following:

    o   takes one or more functions as input

    o   outputs a function

  The **map** function is an example of a higher-order function. It takes as parameters a function *f* and a list of elements, and as the result, returns a new list with *f* applied to each element from the list. **Map** and **reduce** operations can be easily parallelised, meaning that many processors can work simultaneously on part of a dataset without changing or affecting other parts of the data. Higher order functions are therefore a very powerful way of solving problems involving massive amounts of data.

- **Functional programming languages forbid assignment**. In a functional programming language such as Haskell, you cannot write statements such as

  ```
  x = 1
  x = 2
  ```

  This property is known as immutability. An **immutable** object is one whose state cannot be modified after it is created.

  Why is this important for processing across many servers? The answer is that it makes parallel processing extremely easy, because the same function always returns the same result. Given two functions f(x), g(x) in sequence, they can be executed in any order without any possibility that g(x) changes the value of x in a way that changes the result of f(x).

Fact-based model

The fact-based model is an alternative to the relational data model in which immutable facts are recorded with timestamps. This means that data is never deleted and the data set just continues to grow. Because of the timestamps, it is always possible to determine what is current from what is past, i.e. if a fact such as a person's surname changes, the current name can be distinguished from previous names. The fact-based model is particularly suitable for big data because it is very simple and database updates are quick. A graph schema shows how data are represented in the fact-based model, but often (as is the case in this book) the time stamps are omitted for clarity, and only the most recent version of facts are shown, even through all historical versions of them are stored.

Graph schema

The enormous volume of data collected by companies such as Google and Facebook, business enterprises and healthcare organisations typically consist of highly connected entities which are not easily modelled using traditional relational database methods. Instead, graph data structures can be used to represent connected data and to perform analyses on very large datasets.

In a graph database, data is stored as **nodes** and **relationships**, and both nodes and relationships have **properties**. Instead of capturing relationships between entities in a join table as in a relational database, a graph database captures the relationships themselves and their properties directly within the stored data.

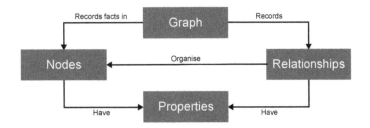

12-72

Example 1

A social network is a good example of a densely connected network. Facebook, which was founded in 2004, had 968 million daily active users in June 2015. Worldwide, they had 1.49 billion monthly active users, approximately 38% of the global population.

The flexibility of the graph model allows new nodes and new relationships to be added without compromising the existing data.

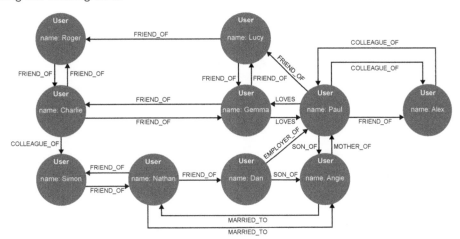

If the data on people and their friends was stored in a relational database, in order to find the answer to the question "Who is friends with Charlie?" we would have to scan the entire dataset looking for friend entries that contained Charlie. With a small dataset, that is straightforward. But now recall the Big O notation, a shorthand way of describing how the performance of the algorithm changes with the size of the dataset. When the dataset doubles, the number of searches doubles – so the algorithm is O(n).

In a graph database, the size of the dataset makes very little difference; we simply have to locate Charlie in the index and follow the links to his friends.

Finding friends-of-friends, or friends-of-friends-of-friends, would be impractical in a relational database, but traversing a graph by following paths makes this task relatively straightforward. Who would know if there is any truth behind the theory of six degrees of separation between any two individuals on earth? Microsoft proved this in 2008 by studying records of 30 billion electronic conversations in 2006, and calculating the chain lengths between 180 billion pairs of users. Any individual user was on average 6.6 hops from another.

> **Q1:** How many degrees of separation are there between Roger and Angie?
>
> **Q2:** Identify some of the nodes, edges and properties of the above graph. (Tip: See chapter 41.)

A graph database will be able to find in a fraction of a second, all friends-of-friends to a depth of say five, whereas a relational database reliant on looking up indexes will take an unacceptably long time.

Example 2

The purchase history of a user can be modelled using a connected graph. In the graph, the user is linked to her orders, and the orders are linked to provide a purchase history.

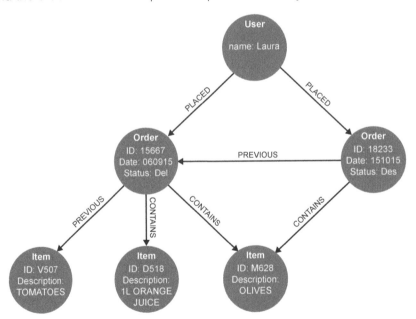

Using the graph, we can see all the orders that a customer has placed, and find what items each order contains. Orders are linked so that order history is easily viewable.

The graph opens up all sorts of useful possibilities. For example, if we find that many users who buy spaghetti also buy coffee beans, we can make a recommendation for coffee beans to purchasers of spaghetti and vice versa. We can add further dimensions to the graph, for example where a customer lives, so that we can find out whether people living in a certain area buy certain products, and then recommend these products to others living in the same area.

Note that there are different ways of drawing these graphs. An alternative way, with the properties written in separate boxes connected to the nodes by dashed lines, is shown in Exercise 4.

Exercises

1. Describe **two** features of functional programming languages which make it easy to write correct and efficient distributed code. [4]

2. List **three** features of a dataset that indicate that a graph schema would be preferable to a relational database for holding the data. In each case, give a reason why this would be the case. [6]

3. "At its core, big data is about predictions." Using two different examples, justify this statement. [6]

4. Big Data can be represented using a graph schema. Data has been collected on families and their occupations. Part of the graph schema is shown below. Complete the graph to show the following facts:

   (a) Bob is the father of Mark (ID 102) and Emma (ID 103). [2]

   (b) Mark is an actor, and Emma is a doctor. [2]

   (c) Gina has a brother Pete (ID 408) who is married to Emma. Pete is a singer. [3]

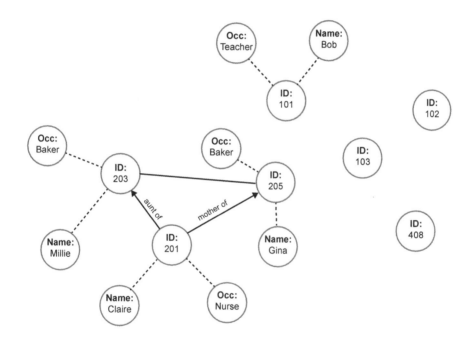

References

Mayer-Schonberger, Viktor and Cukier, Kenneth, "Big Data: A Revolution that will transform how we live, Work and Think", Houghton Mifflin Harcourt Publishing Company, New York, 2013

Miller, Bradley and Ranum, David "Problem solving with algorithms and data structures using Python", Franklin, Beedle and Associates Inc., USA 2011

Robinson, Ian, Webber, Jim and Eifrem, Emil, "Graph databases, 2nd edition" O'Reilly Media Inc., USA 2015

Big data:

http://blog.softwareabstractions.com/the_software_abstractions/2013/06/big-data-and-graph-databases.html

12-72

Appendix A – Floating point form

Objectives

- Know how numbers with a fractional part can be represented in floating point form

- Explain why fixed and floating point representation of decimal numbers may be inaccurate

- Be able to calculate the absolute and relative errors of numerical data stored and processed in computer systems

- Compare absolute and relative errors for large and small magnitude numbers, and numbers close to one

- Compare the advantages and disadvantages of fixed and floating point form in terms of range, precision and speed of calculation

- Be able to normalise un-normalised floating point numbers with positive or negative mantissas

- Explain underflow and overflow and describe the circumstances in which they occur

Revision of fixed point binary numbers

Fixed point binary assumes a pre-determined number of bits before and after the point. This makes fixed point numbers simpler to process but there is a compromise in the range and number of values that can be represented and therefore in the accuracy of representation. Moving the point to the right increases the range but reduces the accuracy of the fractional part and vice versa.

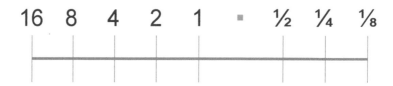

In the example above, only numbers divisible by ⅛ can be represented. The value 4.9, for example would be 'rounded' to 4.875 or 00100111 with three fractional bits to the right of the point.

Q1: Using 1 byte to hold each number with the three least significant bits to the right of the point, convert the following binary numbers to decimal:

    (a) 01010100   (b) 01011101   (c) 00111011   (d) 01010111

Q2: Convert the following numbers to 8-bit binary assuming four bits after the point:

    (a) 2.75   (b) 10.875   (c) 7.5625   (d) 3.4375

Q3: What are the largest and smallest unsigned numbers that can be held in two bytes with four bits after the point? See Figure 1.

Figure 1

Floating point binary numbers

Using 32 bits (4 bytes), the largest fixed point number that can be represented with just one bit after the point is only just over two billion. Floating point binary allows very large numbers to be represented.

When ordinary decimal numbers become very large, they are written in a more convenient scientific notation $m \times 10^n$ where m is known as the **mantissa** or **coefficient**, and n is the exponent or order of magnitude. 5000 can therefore written as 0.5×10^4, and 42,750.254 can be written as 0.42750254×10^5, moving the decimal point five places to the left.

This technique can easily be applied to binary numbers too, where the mantissa and exponent are represented for example using 12 bits, with 8 bits for the mantissa and 4 bits for the exponent. The leftmost bit of both the mantissa and the exponent are sign bits, with 0 indicating a positive number, and 1 a negative number. In a computer, of course, many more bits than this will be used to represent a floating point number, with 32-, 64- and 128-bit floating point numbers all being common.

In all the examples below, eight bits are used for the mantissa and four bits for the exponent. The implied binary point is to the right of the sign bit.

Sign bit		Mantissa							Exponent			
0	•	1	0	1	1	0	1	0	0	0	1	1

$0 \bullet 1011010\ 0011 = 0.101101 \times 2^3 = 0101.101 = 4+1+0.5+0.125 = 5.625$

To convert the floating point binary number above to decimal:

- Write down the mantissa, 0.1011010

- Translate the exponent from binary to decimal 0011 = 3. This means that you have to move the point 3 places to the right, as the mantissa has to be multiplied by 2^3.

- The binary number is therefore 101.1010

- Translate this to binary using the table in Figure 1. The number is 5.625.

> **Q4:** Convert the following floating point numbers to decimal: You can use Figure 1 to help you.
>
> (a) 0 • 1101010 0100   (b) 0 • 1001100 0011

Negative exponents

If the exponent is negative, the decimal point must be moved left instead of right.

$$0 \bullet 1000000\ 1110 = 0.1 \times 2^{-2} = 0.001 = 0.125$$

The example above has a positive mantissa of 0.1000000 and a negative exponent of -2.

- Find the two's complement of the exponent. (Remember that to convert a positive to negative binary number using two's complement you must flip the bits and add 1.) Exponent = -2

- Move the binary point of the mantissa two places to the left, to make it smaller. The mantissa is therefore 0.001 (You can ignore the trailing zeros)

- Translate this to decimal with the help of Figure 1. The answer is 0.125.

> **Q5:** Convert the following floating point number to decimal: 0 • 1100000 1110

Handling negative mantissas

A negative floating point number will have a 1 as the sign bit or MSB (Most Significant Bit) of the mantissa indicating a negative place value.

$$1 \bullet 0101101\ 0101 = -0.1010011 \times 2^5 = -10100.11 = -20.75$$

The example above has a negative mantissa of 1.0101101 and a positive exponent of 0101.

- Find the twos complement of the mantissa. It is 0.1010011, so the bits represent -0.1010011
- Translate the exponent to decimal, 0101 = 5
- Move the binary point 5 places to the right to make it larger. The mantissa is -10100.11
- Translate this to binary with the help of Figure 1. The answer is -20.75.

If the exponent and the mantissa are both negative, the same technique applies, but the point moves to the left instead of the right.

$$1 \bullet 0100000\ 1101 = 1.0100000 \times 2^{-3} = -10.000000 \times 2^{-3} = -.01000000 = -0.25$$

Q6: Convert the following binary numbers to decimal:

(a) 0 • 1000000 1110   (b) 1 • 0011000 0100   (c) 1• 0011000 1111

Normalisation

Normalisation is the process of moving the binary point of a floating point number to provide the maximum level of precision for a given number of bits. This is achieved by ensuring that the first digit after the binary point is a significant digit. To understand this, first consider an example in decimal.

In the decimal system, a number such as $5,842,130_{10}$ can be represented with a 7-digit mantissa in many different ways

$0.584213 \times 10^7 = 5,842,130$

$0.058421 \times 10^8 = 5,842,100$

$0.005842 \times 10^9 = 5,842,000$

The first representation, with a significant (non-zero) digit after the decimal point has the maximum precision.

A number such as 0.00000584213 can be represented as 0.584213×10^{-5}.

Normalising a positive binary number

In binary arithmetic, the leading bit of both mantissa and exponent represent the sign bit.

In normalised floating point form:

A positive number has a sign bit of 0 and the next digit is always 1.

This means that the mantissa of a positive number in normalised form always lies between ½ and 1.

Example 1

Normalise the binary number 0.0001011 0101, held in an 8-bit mantissa and a 4-bit exponent.

- The binary point needs to move 3 places to the right so that there is a 1 following the binary point.
- Making the mantissa larger means we must compensate by making the exponent smaller, so subtract 3 from the exponent, resulting in an exponent of 0010.
- The normalised number is 0.1011000 0010

Normalising a negative binary number

An unnormalised number will have a sign bit of 1 and one or more 1s after the binary point.

Example 2

Normalise the binary number 1.1110111 0001, held in an 8-bit mantissa and a 4-bit exponent.

- Move the binary point right 3 places, so that it is just before the first 0 digit. The mantissa is now 1.0111000
- Moving the binary point to the right makes the number larger, so we must make the exponent smaller to compensate. Subtract 3 from the exponent. The exponent is now $1 - 3 = -2 = 1110$
- The normalised number is 1.0111000 1110

A normalised negative number has a sign bit of 1 and the next bit is always 0.

The mantissa of a negative number in normalised form always lies between -½ and -1.

Example 3

What does the following binary number (with a 5-bit mantissa and a 3-bit exponent) represent in decimal?

-1	1/2	1/4	1/8	1/16	-4	2	1
0	1	1	1	1	0	1	1

This is the largest positive number that can be held using a 5-bit mantissa and a 3-bit exponent, and represents $0.1111 \times 2^3 = 7.5$

Example 4

The most negative number that can be held in a 5-bit mantissa and 3-bit exponent is:

-1	1/2	1/4	1/8	1/16	-4	2	1
1	0	0	0	0	0	1	1

This represents $-1.0000 \times 2^3 = -1000.0 = -8$

Note that the size of the mantissa will determine the **precision** of the number, and the size of the exponent will determine the **range** of numbers that can be held.

Q7: Normalise the following numbers, using an 8-bit mantissa and a 4-bit exponent

(a)   0.0000110 0001

(b)   1.1110011 0011

Converting from decimal to normalised binary floating point

To convert a decimal number to normalised binary floating point, first convert the number to fixed point binary.

Example 5

Convert the number 14.25 to a normalised floating point binary, using an 8-bit mantissa and a 4-bit exponent.

- In fixed point binary, 14.25 = 01110.010

- Remember that the first digit after the sign bit must be 1 in normalised form, so move the binary point 4 places left and increase the exponent from 0 to 4. The number is equivalent to 0.1110010×2^4

- Using a 4-bit exponent, 14.25 = 0 1110010 0100

Example 6

If the decimal number is negative, calculate the twos complement of the fixed point binary:

e.g. Calculate the binary equivalent of -14.25

14.25 = 01110.010

-14.25 = 10001.110 (two's complement)

In normalised form, the first digit after the point must be 0, so the point needs to be moved four places left.

$10001.110 = 1.0001110 \times 2^4 = 10001110\ 0100$

A

> **Q8:** Convert the following numbers to normalised binary floating point numbers, using an 8-bit mantissa and 4-bit exponent:
>
> (a) 16.75   (b) -4.5

Rounding errors

In the decimal system, ⅓ can never be represented completely accurately as a decimal number.

Similarly, some binary numbers cannot be represented in the finite number of bits used to represent them, and other numbers such as 0.1_{10} can never be represented completely accurately in binary. Their accuracy will depend on the number of bits available in fixed point binary, or the size of the mantissa in floating point binary.

Rounding errors are unavoidable and result in a loss of precision.

Example: Using the number line below, find the closest binary representation for the number 0.76₁₀ that can be held in fixed point binary using 8 bits

0.76 is approximately equal to 0.5 + 0.25 + 0.0078125 = 0.7578125

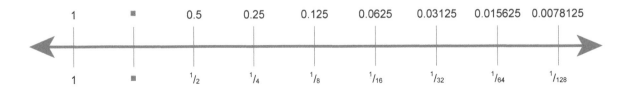

The **absolute error** is calculated as the difference between the number to be represented, and the actual binary number that is the closest possible approximation in the given number of bits.

Absolute error = 0.76 - 0.7578125 = 0.0021875

The **relative error** is the absolute error divided by the number, and may be expressed as a percentage.

Relative error = (0.0021875/0.76) = 0.002878 or 0.2878% (approximately)

> **Q9:** Using the same number line, find the closest binary representation of
>
> (a) 0.1 (b) 0.3333̇ Calculate the absolute and relative errors in each case.

In computer systems reliant on the manipulation of fractional numbers such as foreign currency or stock exchange systems, rounding errors can be expensive. In other systems such as missile guidance and timing, such errors can be fatal.

The effect of number magnitude on absolute and relative errors

An international sprinting track must be exactly 100 metres. What degree of tolerance would be accepted here? 1m? 1cm? 0.1cm or 0.001cm? In fact the IAAF recognise that a tolerance of 2cm or 0.02% is acceptable. 2cm is the **absolute error** above or below an actual track length, and 0.02% is the **relative error**, relative to the official length.

Depending on the application and the magnitude of the numbers, the significance or implications of an absolute or relative error can change. A relative margin of error of only 0.0005 on an estimated drilling depth of 32,000ft might seem small, but not when you find you are an absolute 16ft short of drilling pipe on board an oil platform in the middle of the sea. Notice that absolute errors are always a positive difference between the actual or recorded data.

An absolute error of say 0.5 in a number of 10,000 is a relative error of 0.005%. The same error in a number close to 1, say 0.99, is approximately 50.5%; clearly very much more significant.

In a very small number, for example 0.00001, a seemingly very small absolute error of 0.000005 is a relative error of 50%.

Application	Published data	Recorded data	Absolute error	Relative error
Currency exchange rate	1.35264 Euros to GBP	1.35 Euros to GBP	0.00264	0.20%
Train times	18 minutes	19 minutes	1 minute	5.56%
Offshore oil drilling depth	32,000 feet	32,016 feet	16 feet	0.05%

Fixed point vs floating point

Fixed and floating point each have their own advantages and disadvantages in terms of range, precision and the speed of calculation.

- Floating point allows a far greater range of numbers using the same number of bits. Very large numbers and very small fractional numbers can be represented. The larger the mantissa, the greater the precision, and the larger the exponent, the greater the range.

- In fixed point binary, the range and precision of numbers that can be represented depends on the position of the binary point. The more digits to the left of the point, the greater the range, but the lower the precision. For example, referring to Figure 1, if the binary point in a 16-bit number is placed four places from the least significant bit, numbers are only precise to four binary places. A decimal number such as 12.53125 cannot be accurately represented. In floating point, it can be represented with absolute precision as, say, 011001000100 0100.

- Fixed point binary is a simpler system and is faster to process.

Underflow and overflow

Underflow occurs when a number is too small to be represented in the allotted number of bits. If, for example, a very small number is divided by another number greater than 1, underflow may occur and the result will be represented by 0.

Overflow occurs when the result of a calculation is too large to be held in the number of bits allocated.

Exercises

1. A normalised floating point representation uses an 8-bit mantissa and a 4-bit exponent, both stored using **two's complement format**.

   (a) In binary, write in the boxes below, the smallest positive number that can be represented using this normalised floating point system.

   Mantissa   Exponent   [2]

   (b) This is a floating point representation of a number:

   | 1 | 0 | 1 | 1 | 0 | 0 | 0 | 0 | | 0 | 0 | 1 | 0 |

   Mantissa   Exponent   [2]

   Calculate the decimal number. Show your working.   [2]

   (c) Write the normalised representation of the decimal value 12.75 in the boxes below:

   Mantissa   Exponent   [2]

   (d) Floating point numbers are usually stored in normalised form.

   State two advantages of using a normalised representation.   [2]

   (e) An alternative **two's complement format** representation is proposed. In the alternative representation **7 bits** will be used to store the mantissa and **5 bits** will be used to store the exponent.

   Existing representation (8-bit mantissa, 4-bit exponent):

   Mantissa   Exponent

   Proposed alternative representation (7-bit mantissa, 5-bit exponent):

   Mantissa   Exponent   [2]

   Explain the effects of using the proposed alternative representation instead of the existing representation.   [2]

AQA Unit 3 Qu 3 June 2011

Appendix B – Adders and D-type flip-flops

Objectives

- Recognise and trace the logic of the circuits of a half-adder and a full-adder
- Construct the circuit for a half-adder
- Be familiar with the use of the edge-triggered D-type flip-flop as a memory unit

Performing calculations using gates

With the right combination of gates, it is possible to output the result of a binary addition or subtraction including the value of any carry bit as a second output.

Half-adders

A half-adder can take an input of two bits and give a two-bit output as the correct result of an addition of the two inputs.

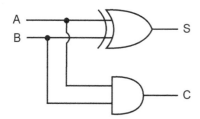

A		B		S	C
0	+	0	=	0	0
0	+	1	=	1	0
1	+	0	=	1	0
1	+	1	=	0	1

This is shown by the diagram above and represented by the truth table where S represents the sum and C represents the carry bit. S can be given as $S = A \oplus B$, and C as $C = A \cdot B$. Although a half-adder can output the value of a carry bit, it only has two inputs so it cannot use the carry from a previous addition as a third input to a subsequent addition in order to add n-bit numbers.

Full adders

A full adder combines two half-adders to add three bits together including the two inputs A and B, and a carry bit C. The logic gate circuit below illustrates how two half-adders have been connected with an additional OR gate to output the carry bit.

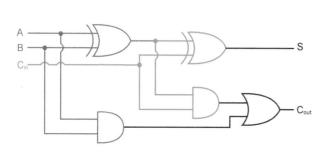

A		B		C_{in}		S	C_{out}
0	+	0	+	0	=	0	0
0	+	0	+	1	=	1	0
0	+	1	+	0	=	1	0
0	+	1	+	1	=	0	1
1	+	0	+	0	=	1	0
1	+	0	+	1	=	0	1
1	+	1	+	0	=	0	1
1	+	1	+	1	=	1	1

Now the Boolean logic becomes $S = A \oplus B \oplus C_{in}$, and $C_{out} = (A \cdot B) + (C_{in} \cdot (A \oplus B))$.

Concatenating full adders

Multiple full adders can be connected together. Using this construct, n full adders can be connected together in order to input the carry bit into a subsequent adder along with two new inputs to create a concatenated adder capable of adding a binary number of n bits.

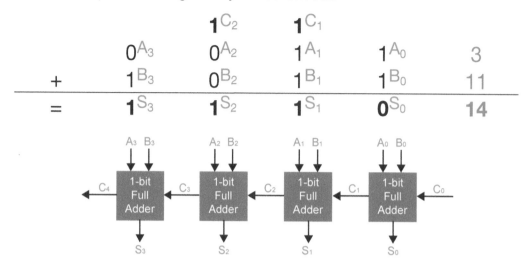

$$
\begin{array}{ccccccc}
 & & & \mathbf{1}^{C_2} & \mathbf{1}^{C_1} & & \\
 & 0^{A_3} & 0^{A_2} & 1^{A_1} & 1^{A_0} & & 3 \\
+ & 1^{B_3} & 0^{B_2} & 1^{B_1} & 1^{B_0} & & 11 \\
\hline
= & \mathbf{1}^{S_3} & \mathbf{1}^{S_2} & \mathbf{1}^{S_1} & 0^{S_0} & & 14 \\
\end{array}
$$

> **Q1:** What would be the output S_4 from a fifth adder connected to the diagram above if the inputs for A_4 and B_4 were 0 and 1? What would be the output C_5?

D-type flip-flops

A flip-flop is an elemental **sequential logic circuit** that can store one bit and flip between two states, 0 and 1. It has two inputs, a control input labelled D and a clock signal.

The **clock** or **oscillator** is another type of sequential circuit that changes state at regular time intervals. Clocks are needed to synchronise the change of state of flip-flop circuits.

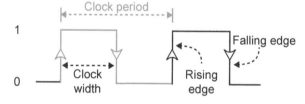

The **D-type flip-flop** (D stands for Data or Delay) is a positive **edge-triggered flip-flop**, meaning that it can only change the output value from 1 to 0 or vice versa when the clock is at a rising or positive edge, i.e. at the beginning of a clock period.

When the clock is not at a positive edge, the input value is held and does not change. **The flip-flop circuit is important because it can be used as a memory cell to store the state of a bit.**

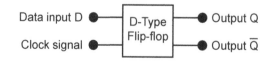

Output Q only takes on a new value if the value at D has changed at the point of a clock pulse. This means that the clock pulse will freeze or 'store' the input value at D until the next clock pulse. If D remains the same on the next clock pulse, the flip-flop will hold the same value.

The use of a D-type flip-flop as a memory unit

A flip-flop comprises several NAND (or AND and OR) gates and is effectively 1-bit memory. To store eight bits, eight flip-flops are required. **Register memories** are constructed by connecting a series of flip-flops in a row and are typically used for the intermediate storage needed during arithmetic operations. Static RAM is also created using D-type flip-flops. Imagine trying to assemble 16GB of memory in this way!

The graph below illustrates how the output Q only changes to match the input D in response to the rising edge on the clock signal. Q therefore delays, or 'stores' the value of D by up to one clock cycle.

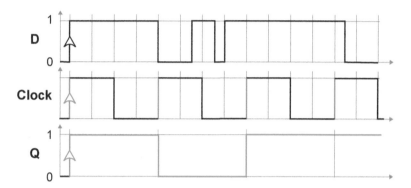

Exercises

1. A half-adder is used to find the sum of the addition of two binary digits.

(a) Complete the diagram below to construct a half adder circuit.   [1]

(b) Complete the following truth table for a half adder's outputs S and C.

A	B	S	C

[2]

(c) How does a full adder differ from a half adder in terms of its inputs?   [2]

B

2. An edge-triggered D-type flip-flop can be used as a memory cell to store the value of a single bit. The following graph shows the clock cycle and the input signals applied to D.

(a)   Label each rising edge on the diagram below.   [1]

(b)   Draw the flip-flop's output Q on the graph.   [4]

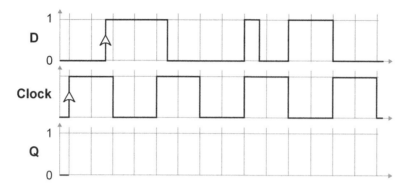

Index

Index

Index

Lightning Source UK Ltd.
Milton Keynes UK
UKOW07f1518140616

276286UK00010B/34/P